D1154129

JONATHAN SWIFT

Poetry & Prose

With appreciations by

POPE, JOHNSON, SCOTT

HAZLITT

and others

With an Introduction and Notes by

HERBERT DAVIS

OXFORD

AT THE CLARENDON PRESS

1964

Oxford University Press, Amen House, London E.C.4

GLASGOW NEW YORK TORONTO MELBOURNE WELLINGTON
BOMBAY CALCUTTA MADRAS KARACHI LAHORE DACCA
CAPE TOWN SALISBURY NAIROBI IBADAN ACCRA
KUALA LUMPUR HONG KONG

PRINTED IN GREAT BRITIAN
AT THE UNIVERSITY PRESS, OXFORD
BY VIVIAN RIDLER
PRINTER TO THE UNIVERSITY

CONTENTS

INTRODUCTION

SWIFT is a writer whose genius and powers have never been in doubt but whose character and work have always been the subject of very divided opinions. He inspired the warmest affection among his friends; but he was bitterly hated and feared and calumniated by his enemies. After his death, while his writings continued to be printed and read, the judgements of his critics varied from the adulations of his publishers, who boasted that he was 'one of the greatest Patriots and Genius's, and the most correct Writer of this or any other Age', to the unsparing condemnation of the *Edinburgh Review* in 1816: 'We think there are not many of those who have served a regular apprenticeship to corruption and jobbing, who could go through their task with more coolness and hardihood than this pious neophyte.' This may be regarded as merely the expression of party prejudice; but Victorians like Thackeray and Masson went much further in denouncing his whole work as a foul and hateful attack upon humanity. Thackeray describes him as 'a monster gibbering shrieks, and gnashing imprecations against mankind . . . filthy in word, filthy in thought, furious, raging, obscene'. Masson explains that he was possessed of the devil; Swift's 'communion with the invisible was almost exclusively on the infernal side—that consciousness of chains wound round his own moving frame at one end, and at the other tugged at by demons in the depths of their populous pit, etc., etc.' In the twentieth century he was more coolly examined by experts like Havelock Ellis and writers like Aldous Huxley and D. H. Lawrence, who note 'the intensity, the almost insane violence of that "hatred of bowels" which is the essence of his misanthropy and which underlies the whole of his work'.

His own contemporaries do not seem to have made any

such startling discoveries. Addison, who is reputed to have been an observant spectator of men and manners in the early years of the eighteenth century, described him as 'the most agreeable companion, the truest friend, and the greatest genius of his age'. Pope, in dedicating *The Dunciad* to him in 1729, addressed him thus:

> O Thou! whatever title please thine ear,
> Dean, Drapier, Bickerstaff, or Gulliver!
> Whether thou chuse Cervantes' serious air,
> Or laugh and shake in Rabelais' easy chair
> Or praise the Court, or magnify Mankind,
> Or thy griev'd Country's copper chains unbind;

Such a description serves to remind us of the variety of Swift, the many roles he chose to assume, the different causes he fought for; but, above all, it recognizes his place in the great European tradition of humour and satire, by the side of Rabelais and Cervantes.

His reputation as a wit and as a satirist of genius was first fully revealed in *A Tale of a Tub,* published together with *The Battle of the Books,* in 1704. Here he sees himself as holding up a sort of mirror, in which his victims—the false pretenders to learning and religion—may behold what they really look like; though he is already sufficiently experienced in the ways of the world to know that the beholders will discover in it everybody's face but their own. Nevertheless he succeeded in rousing some of them to anger, particularly by his exposure of the extravagances of the Roman Church and the cant of the sects; and it is not surprising that his Rabelaisian ribaldry shocked the authorities of the Established Church, whom he professed to be defending. For, even though it can be shown that in the main fable concerned with the tale of the three brothers, Peter and Martin and Jack, Swift is no rougher than many of the seventeenth-century defenders of the Anglican Church, yet the tone of the book as a whole is such that most readers will be more aware of the destructive force of its satire and the unrestrained play of the wit in exposing the delusions and absurdities connected with religion, than of the ardour of one primarily concerned with the defence of orthodoxy. In the Apology which he wrote for the fifth edition of the book in 1710, Swift tried to justify his preoccupation with ridiculing the corruptions of religion by claiming that 'the tritest Maxim in the World' teaches us 'that Religion being the best of Things, its Corruptions are likely to be the worst'.

At the same time he was preparing to bring out a volume of *Miscellanies in Prose and Verse* which would contain some unexceptionable writings on politics and religion. 'A Project for the Advancement of Religion' takes the form of a direct appeal from 'a Person of Quality' to the Queen to exert all the influence of the Court against the enemies of religion and the Church—the men of pleasure, the free-thinkers, and the 'low Party' who 'rattle it out against Priestcraft and High Church'. Another essay is one of his neatest and most perfect ironies, in which the tone set so precisely in the title is maintained exactly throughout the piece—'An Argument to prove that the Abolishing of Christianity in England, May as things now stand, be attended with some Inconveniences, and perhaps not produce those many good Effects proposed thereby'. There can be no doubt about the seriousness of his purpose to support the Established Church, and in particular to oppose those who advocated the repeal of the Test Act, by which all in public office were required to accept its doctrines and practices. The Argument is carried on in the form of a series of logical and rational propositions in defence of nominal Christianity, and is maintained in such a way as to take into account the prejudices of the most enlightened freethinker and provide opportunity for irony at his expense:

I hope, no Reader imagines me so weak to stand up in the Defence of *real* Christianity; such as used in primitive Times (if we may believe the Authors of those Ages) to have an Influence upon Mens Belief and Actions: To offer at the Restoring of that, would indeed be a wild Project; . . .

Throughout the volume we find the same mind at work as in *A Tale of a Tub* with its dislike of cant and hypocrisy, its distrust of all romantic notions of religious or poetic inspiration. It had driven him as a young man to give up his attempts to imitate the fashion for panegyric verse and Pindaric odes, and had taught him to scorn the Muse, whom he had found to be but a wild form dependent on the brain,

> Troubling the crystal fountain of the sight,
> Which darts on poets eyes a trembling light;
> Kindled while reason sleeps, but quickly flies
> Like antic shapes in dreams, from waking eyes:

It led him now to employ his skill in rhyming to make us look at the things which are happening immediately around us, amusing and trivial like the chatter in the servants' hall, or drab and unpleasant, as in those verses he had sent to Steele for his *Tatler*, which were a parody of the pastoral and the picturesque, cataloguing in vivid detail what he had observed in the streets of the city in the early hours of the morning or during a heavy shower.

Thus, by 1710, when he was forty-three, he had established his reputation as a genius, and as a writer of great power both in verse and prose. When, shortly afterwards, he was persuaded to turn this to account in political controversy, in support of the Tory ministry during the last years of the reign of Queen Anne, he was able to use the same methods to expose the hollowness of the military glories of Marlborough's great victories, which did nothing to bring the war to an end and continued to add to the enormous national debt. With the same rational arguments, the same air of clarity, and often with the same irony, he was able to convince his readers that they had been deceived; and that the only sensible thing to do was to make peace with France as soon as possible. Years later, at the time of the death of Marlborough, he could not resist the temptation to point the moral by providing for his funeral a satirical Elegy. There is no better example of the ruthlessness of Swift, of the violence he can put into a contemptuous line, yet at the same time preserving the calm and awful dignity of a judge, required by his office to pronounce judgement. His imagination is stirred by the fervour of his feelings and nothing is left of malice or personal vindictiveness, as he finds the perfect image to reveal the emptiness of all the honours that this world can give:

> Come hither, all ye empty things,
> Ye bubbles rais'd by breath of Kings;
> Who float upon the tide of state,
> Come hither, and behold your fate.

This was written at the height of his powers, when he was in the middle of his composition of *Gulliver's Travels*, when he had been settled for eight years in Dublin, as Dean of St. Patrick's, and had already begun a second political campaign in which he was to appear as the champion of Ireland, in her attempt to remove some of the restrictions upon her trade, imposed on her by the English government. In that campaign the source of his power is again derived from the anger which stirred him at the spectacle of the miseries of the people of Ireland and his fury at their slavish spirit in tolerating them. In his *Proposal for the Universal Use of Irish Manufactures*, he had reminded them of Ovid's fable of Arachne, turned into a spider by Pallas and condemned to 'spin and weave for ever out of her own bowels', only to point out that their fate was worse:

> For the greatest Part of our Bowels and vitals is extracted, without allowing us the Liberty of spinning and weaving them.

Then he quotes the Scriptures to them—'Oppression makes a wise Man mad'—and expounds them, as it was his duty to do, drawing out the consequences very logically:

. . . the Reason why some Men are not *mad,* is because they are not *wise*: However, it were to be wished that *Oppression* would, in Time, teach a little *Wisdom* to *Fools.*

Here are the same telling images, the same inescapable logic. And when he comes to write the *Drapier's Letters,* the same imaginative power, stirred by the depth of his feelings, is at work, prompting him suddenly to transform himself into the figure of David, armed only with a sling, in his fight against the heavy-armed giant Goliath. He will likewise stand forth before his people, as one chosen to save them from their adversary, and like David, assured of victory against all odds. His overweening confidence rests upon his contempt for the powers of this world. In the presence of such stupidity and folly he feels himself, like Gulliver among the Lilliputians, able to challenge the authority of the whole government:

Let whoever think otherwise, I M. B. *Drapier,* desire to be excepted. For I declare . . . I am so far from *depending* upon the People of England, that, if they should ever *rebel* against my Sovereign, (which God forbid) I would be ready at the first Command from his Majesty to take Arms against them;

But in spite of the triumph of the Drapier and the influence he continued to have over the people of Dublin, and the satisfaction that gave him, he was not deceived; he knew that he could never put an end to the miseries of Ireland. He could, however, draw up a 'Modest Proposal' which might prove a remedy, calculated for Ireland alone and for no other Kingdom that ever was or could be on earth; one that at the same time would be entirely unexceptionable, because there would be 'no possible danger in it of *disobliging* England'. His proposal was a very simple one, which would reduce the population and provide a little money for poor families. Let a hundred thousand children be offered for sale at a year old, 'well fattened for a good table'. All the obvious objections that could possibly be brought against such a proposal are very quietly and adequately put aside, and the solid advantages are reckoned up. A large number of other proposals are considered, but these are all rejected as none of them affording 'a Glimpse of Hope, that there will ever be some hearty and sincere Attempt to put them in Practice'. This was almost Swift's last word on Ireland. But later it occurred to him that there was one thing he could himself do, which might be of some use. He mentions it at the end of his *Verses on the Death of Dr. Swift,* before he actually made the necessary provisions in his will:

> He gave the little Wealth he had,
> To build a House for Fools and Mad:
> And shew'd by one satyric Touch,
> No Nation wanted it so much.

It would be an error, however, to imagine for a moment that the Dean of St. Patrick's entirely immersed himself in Irish affairs. He had remained in touch with his friends in England, and had spent a great deal of time writing his memoirs, and preparing a history of English politics during the period he had taken part in them. When, after an absence of twelve years he returned in 1726 to spend the summer with Arbuthnot and Pope and Gay, and make acquaintance again with Court circles, he brought with him the manuscript of a book which he had written 'to vex the world'; and before he returned to Ireland, he sent it to be printed. When it appeared that winter, *Gulliver's Travels* was an immediate success. It was read with delight by the victims of his satire; and Dr. Arbuthnot wrote to congratulate him that at his age he could produce 'such a merry work'.

Such a reception may have been due in part to the discretion of his London publisher, who had removed or toned down some of the most violent invective against Kings and their ministers, the nobility and men of quality, lawyers, and judges. But he had not altered anything in Gulliver's account of the Yahoos or the Struldbrugs; he had done nothing to disguise his enthusiasm for the Houyhnhnms and his detestation for the human animal, when he had been forced to return home after his eyes had been opened by his experience among those four-footed rationalists. He had left the full effect of Swift's general indictment of humanity—the exposure of all its littlenesses and childish follies as reflected in the society of the tiny people of Lilliput; the misuses of reason and intelligence, as manifested in the works of the learned, whether they are, as in Laputa, occupied with scientific experiments or with judgements on the characters of men and events in past history; the terrible denunciation of man's inhumanity to man, delivered with such effect by his gigantic highness, the King of Brobdingnag; and the final parody of man's physical nature in those horrible beasts, the Yahoos, which many later readers found it so difficult to stomach.

The latest way of escape from these intolerable slanders is to follow the modern critics, who tell us that we must not be so foolish as to identify Swift with Gulliver, and to imagine that he shares Gulliver's admiration for the Houyhnhnms, or his horrifying discovery of the likeness between the Yahoos and himself and his family. Gulliver, we are told, is a character in the book, who changes and develops under the influence of the things that happen to him in his voyages. He is not only the narrator, but is created by his author to play a part in the action of the book; we must no more expect to find the meaning of the book in the opinions he expresses than we should to find the meaning of the play stated by one of the characters.

But *Gulliver's Travels* is not a play or a novel; its form is modelled on Dampier's *Voyages*. It was intended in part to be a parody of the popular reading of the moment, the travellers' tales, the sort of 'trash' that Swift himself delighted in. They might provide tall stories of strange monsters and untamed or innocent savages, but Gulliver's voyages took him to even more remote places, to those farthest shores and coasts still uncharted on the latest maps, where he could be expected to meet with marvellous adventures, as magnificent or as comic as anything in Rabelais or Cervantes. In Lilliput we see him, a Gargantuan figure, striding over the city walls, and lying down on his side in order to get a glimpse of the magnificence of the royal palace, or wading through the ocean that divides that country from its neighbours, drawing after him the whole of the enemies' fleet; or a tiny creature among the giants, carried off in the arms of a huge monkey which capers with him on to the roof, holding him tight in his arms and stuffing food into his mouth. His adventurous spirit seems prepared for anything to happen, and he quickly learns to adapt himself to the ways of life among those gentle civilized horses, and to find pleasure in the company of the sorrel mare. He is only ill at ease among the strange inhabitants of Laputa; but there is horror enough in his discovery of the Struldbrugs who cannot die, and in his realization that the Yahoos could mistake him for one of their own species.

All this superb play of the creative imagination, however, is directed by Swift's intention to make us share his view of the grim comedy of human life. He takes us up in his hands like the giant king of Brobdingnag, and strokes us gently, diverting us with all the fun and merriment, while he tells us his final conclusion that, on the whole, we are 'the most pernicious Race of little odious Vermin that Nature ever suffered to crawl upon the Surface of the Earth'. He said he wanted to vex us, to make it impossible for us to be blind to our real condition, to stir us out of our complacencies. He has no hope of our reformation ; nor is it his business to offer us any comfort. He must remain to the end a satirist, railing at our stupidities and our vices, our blindness, and our foolish pride. For, like Gulliver, who had learnt by the instructions of his illustrious master in Houyhnhnmland, he had rid himself of 'that infernal Habit of Lying, Shuffling, Deceiving, and equivocating, so deeply rooted in the very Souls of all my Species'—and he could only speak the truth.

Perhaps he was content to think that some of his readers might learn from his book to imitate him in this ; for he was willing to admit that it had been written

> As with a moral View design'd
> To cure the Vices of Mankind.

LIFE

1667 Born in Dublin 30 Nov., some months after his father's death.

1673 Sent to the best school in Ireland, at Kilkenny.

1682 Entered Trinity College, Dublin.

1686 B.A. *speciali gratia.*

1689 Joined his mother in England, having left Dublin on the outbreak of the war in Ireland.
Later entered the household of Sir William Temple.

1690 Returned to Ireland.

1691 Came back to England in the summer and later joined Temple again at Moor Park, where Stella was then a child of ten. *Ode to the Athenian Society* printed; other Odes written during the next two years, but unpublished.

1692 M.A. Oxford.

1694 Ordained in Ireland and appointed to prebend of Kilroot.

1696 Returned to Moor Park.

1699 Death of Sir William Temple; Swift returned to Ireland as domestic chaplain to the Earl of Berkeley.

1700 Vicar of Laracor and prebend of St. Patrick's, Dublin. Published *Letters of Sir William Temple*, in 2 vols.

1701 *A Discourse of the Contests and Dissensions between the Nobles and Commons in Athens and Rome etc.* published.

1702 D.D. of Trinity College, Dublin.

1704 *A Tale of a Tub* and *The Battle of the Books* published.

1707–9 In London. *Bickerstaffe Papers* published. Friend of Addison and Steele.

1709 *A Project for the Advancement of Religion* published. Returned to Ireland in June.

1710 Arrived in London in Sept., with authority from the Church of Ireland to seek the remission of First Fruits from Queen Anne. Well received by Harley; put in charge of the Tory paper, the *Examiner*. Full account in *Journal to Stella*, 1710–13.

1711 *Miscellanies in Prose and Verse* published.

1712 *Conduct of the Allies* published.

1713 Installed Dean of St. Patrick's, Dublin, 13 June.

1714 Returned to Ireland after the death of Queen Anne, 1 Aug. Devotes himself to his duties as Dean, and to work on his Memoirs of the last four years, which remained unpublished till after his death.

1720 *A Proposal for the Universal Use of Irish Manufactures* published.

1721 At work on *Gulliver's Travels.*

1724 The *Drapier's Letters* published. His triumph as Hibernian Patriot.

1726 Visit to London; with Arbuthnot and Pope. *Gulliver's Travels* published on 28 Oct., after Swift's return to Dublin.

1727 Last visit to England.

1728 Death of Stella, 28 Jan. Contributes to the *Intelligencer*.

1729 *A Modest Proposal* published.

1731 Working at *Polite Conversation* and *Directions to Servants*. Also *Verses on the Death of Dr. Swift* and other poems.

1732 Tracts on the Test Act and Irish affairs.

1735 *Collected Works* in four vols., printed by Faulkner in Dublin.

1738 *Polite Conversation* published in London. *Collected Works*, vols. 5 and 6, published in Dublin.

1742 Found to be 'of unsound mind and memory'.

1745 Died 19 Oct.

APPRECIATIONS

JOSEPH ADDISON ON SWIFT

From Addison's letter to Swift, 1 Oct. 1718

I LIVE still in hopes of seeing you in England and if you woud take my House at Bilton in your way which lies upon the Road within a Mile of Rugby I woud strain hard to meet you there provided you woud make me happy in your Company for some Days. The greatest pleasure I have met with for some months is in the conversation of my old friend D[r] Smalridge who since the Death of the Excellent man you mention is to me the most candid and agreeable of all Bishops, I woud say clergymen, were not Deans comprehended under that Title. We have often talkd of you and when I assure you he has an Exquisite taste of writing I need not tell you how he talks on such a Subject. I look upon it as my good fortune that I can expresse my Esteem of You even to those who are not of the Bishop's party without giving Offence. When a man has so much Compass in his character he affords his friends topicks enough to enlarge upon that all sides admire. I am sure a sincere and zealous friendly Behaviour distinguishes you as much as your many more shining talents, and as I have received particular Instances of it you must have a very bad opinion of me if you do not think I heartily Love and respect you and that I am Ever, Dear Sir | Your most Obedient | and most Humble Servant | J. Addison.

DR. JOHN ARBUTHNOT ON SWIFT

From Arbuthnot's letters to Swift, 17 Oct. 1725 and 5 Nov. 1726

THE hopes of seeing once more the Dean of St patricks revives my spirits, I can not help imagining some of our old club mett together like Mariners after a Storm. for gods sake don't tantalize your freinds, any more. I can prove by twenty unanswerable arguments that it is absolutely necessary, that yow should come over to England, that it would be committing the greatest absurdity that ever was not to do it the next approaching Winter. I beleive indeed it is just possible to save your soul wtout it & thats all. As for your Book, (of which I have framd to my self, such an idea, that I am persuaded ther is no doing any good upon mankind without it) I will sett the letters my self rather than that it should not be publish'd. but before yow putt the finishing hand to it it is really necessary to be acquainted wth some new improvements of mankind that have appeared of late and are dayly appearing. Mankind has an inexhaustible source of invention in the way of folly, & madness. I have only one fear, that when yow come over yow will be so much cuveted & taken up by the Ministry, that unless your freind's meett you at their tables, they will have none of Your company: this is really no joke; I am quite in earnest. Your deafness is so necessary a thing, that I allmost begin to think it is an affectation. I remember yow usd to reckon dinners I know of near half a years dinner's where you are allready bespoke. It is worth your while to come to see our old freind Lewis who is wiser than ever he was the best of husbands. I am sure I can say from my own experience, that he is the best of freind's he was so to me when he had little hope I should ever live to thank him. Yow must acquaint me before yow take [your] jurney, that we may provide a convenient Lodging for yow amongst your Freinds. I am call'd away this moment, & have only time to add that I long to see yow, & am most sincerely, Dr Sir Your most faithfull humble servt | Jo: Arbuthnott.

I take it mighty kindly that a man of your high post, Dear Sir, was pleased to write me so long a letter. I look upon the captain Tom of a great Nation to be a much greater Man than the Governour of it.

I am sorry your commission about your singer has not been executed sooner, it is not Nanny's Fault, who has spoke severall times to Dr Pepush about it, & wrote three or four letters, & received for answer that he would write for the young fellow; but still nothing is done, I will endeavour to gett his name & direction & write to him my self.

Your books shall be sent as directed; they have been printed above a month, but I cannot gett my subscribers' names. I will make over all my profits to you, for the property of Gulliver's Travells, which I believe, will have as 10 great a Run as John Bunian. Gulliver is a happy man that at his age can write such a merry work.

I made my Lord ArchBishop's compliment to her R Highness who returns his Grace her thanks, at the same time Mrs Howard Read your letter to herself. The princess immediately seizd on your plade for her own use, & has orderd the young Princesses to be clad in the same. when I had the honor to see her She was Reading Gulliver, & was just come to the passage of the Hobbling prince, which she laughed at. I tell yow freely the part of the projectors is the 20 least Brilliant. Lewis Grumbles a little at it & says he wants the Key to it, & is dayly refining.

Gulliver is in every body's Hands Lord Scarborow who is no inventor of Storys told me that he fell in company with a Master of a ship, who told him that he was very well acquainted with Gulliver, but that the printer had Mistaken, that he livd in Wapping, & not in Rotherhith. I lent the Book to an old Gentleman, who went immediately to his Map to search for Lilly putt.

JOHN GAY ON SWIFT

From Gay's letter to Swift, 17 Nov. 1726

ABOUT ten days ago a Book was publish'd here of the 30 Travels of one Gulliver, which hath been the conversation

of the whole town ever since: The whole impression sold in a week; and nothing is more diverting than to hear the different opinions people give of it, though all agree in liking it extreamly. 'Tis generally said that you are the Author, but I am told, the Bookseller declares he knows not from what hand it came. From the highest to the lowest it is universally read, from the Cabinet-council to the Nursery. The Politicians to a man agree, that it is free from particular reflections, but that the Satire on general societies of men is
10 too severe. Not but we now and then meet with people of greater perspicuity, who are in search for particular applications in every leaf; and it is highly probable we shall have keys published to give light into Gulliver's design. Your Lord —— is the person who least approves it, blaming it as a design of evil consequence to depreciate human nature, at which it cannot be wondered that he takes most offence, being himself the most accomplish'd of his species, and so losing more than any other of that praise which is due both to the dignity and virtue of a man. Your friend, my Lord
20 Harcourt, commends it very much, though he thinks in some places the matter too far carried. The Duchess Dowager of Marlborough is in raptures at it; she says she can dream of nothing else since she read it; she declares, that she hath now found out, that her whole life hath been lost in caressing the worst part of mankind, and treating the best as her foes; and that if she knew Gulliver, tho' he had been the worst enemy she ever had, she would give up all her present acquaintance for his friendship. You may see by this, that you are not much injur'd by being suppos'd the
30 Author of this piece. If you are, you have disoblig'd us, and two or three of your best friends, in not giving us the least hint of it while you were with us; and in particular Dr. Arbuthnot, who says it is ten thousand pitys he had not known it, he could have added such abundance of things upon every subject. Among Lady-critics, some have found

out that Mr. Gulliver had a particular malice to maids of honour. Those of them who frequent the Church, say, his design is impious, and that it is an insult on Providence, by depreciating the works of the Creator. Notwithstanding I am told the Princess hath read it with great pleasure. As to other Critics, they think the flying island is the least entertaining; and so great an opinion the town have of the impossibility of Gulliver's writing at all below himself, that 'tis agreed that Part was not writ by the same Hand, tho' this hath its defenders too. It hath pass'd Lords and Commons, 10 *nemine contradicente*; and the whole town, men, women, and children are quite full of it.

Perhaps I may all this time be talking to you of a Book you have never seen, and which hath not yet reach'd Ireland; if it hath not, I believe what we have said will be sufficient to recommend it to your reading, and that you order me to send it to you.

But it will be much better to come over your self, and read it here, where you will have the pleasure of variety of commentators, to explain the difficult passages to you. 20

We all rejoyce that you have fixt the precise time of your coming to be *cum hirundine prima*; which we modern naturalists pronounce, ought to be reckon'd, contrary to Pliny in this northern latitude of fifty-two degrees, from the end of February, Styl. Greg. at farthest. But to us your friends, the coming of such a black swallow as you, will make a summer in the worst of seasons. We are no less glad at your mention of Twickenham and Dawley; and in town you know you have a lodging at Court.

The Princess is cloath'd in Irish silk; pray give our ser- 30 vice to the Weavers. We are strangely surpriz'd to hear that the Bells in Ireland ring without your money; I hope you do not write the thing that is not. We are afraid that B— hath been guilty of that crime, that you (like a Houyhnhnm) have treated him as a Yahoo, and discarded him your service. I fear you do not understand these modish terms, which every creature now understands but your self.

You tell us your Wine is bad, and that the Clergy do not frequent your house, which we look upon to be tautology. The best advice we can give you is, to make them a present of your wine, and come away to better.

You fancy we envy you, but you are mistaken, we envy those you are with, for we cannot envy the man we love. Adieu.

ALEXANDER POPE ON SWIFT

From Pope's letters to Swift, Aug. 1723 and 15 Oct. 1725

It is an honest Truth, there's no one living or dead of whom I think oft'ner, or better than yourself. I look upon You to be, (as to me) in a State between both: you have from me all the passions, & good wishes, that can attend the Living; & all that Respect & tender Sense of Loss, that we feel for the Dead. Whatever you seem to think of your withdrawn & separate State, at this distance, & in this absence, Dr Swift lives still in England, in ev'ry place & company where he woud chuse to live; & I find him in all the conversations I keep, & in all the Hearts in which I would have any Share. We have never met these many Years without mention of you.

I am wonderfully pleas'd with the suddenness of your kind answer. It makes me hope you are coming towards us, and that you incline [more and more] toward your old friends in proportion as you draw nearer to them; in short, that you are getting into Our Vortex. Here is one, who was once a powerful Planet [Lord Bol.] who has now (after long experience of all that comes of shining) learn'd to be content with returning to his First point, without the thought or ambition of shining at all. Here is another, who thinks one of the greatest Glories of his Father was to have distinguish'd and Lov'd you, and who loves you hereditarily. Here is Arbuthnot, [yet living,] recover'd from the jaws of death, and more pleas'd with the hope of seeing you again, than of reviving a world he has long despis'd every part of, but what is made up of a few men like yourself. He goes abroad again, and is more chearful than even Health can make a man, for he has a good Conscience into the bargain (which is the most *Catholick* of all Remedies, tho not the most *Universal*) I knew it would be a pleasure to you to hear this; and in 10 truth, that made me write so soon to you.

I have often imagined to myself, that if ever All of us met again, after so many Varieties and Changes, after so much of the Old world, and of the Old man in each of us, had been alter'd; [after there has been a New Heaven, and a New Earth, in our Minds, and bodies,] that Scarce a single thought of the one any more than a single atome of the other, remains just the same: I've fancy'd, I say, that we shou'd meet like the Righteous in the Millennium, quite in peace, divested of all our former passions, smiling at all our own 20 designs, and content to enjoy the Kingdome of the Just in Tranquillity. But I find you would rather be employ'd as an Avenging Angel of wrath, to break your Vial of Indignation over the heads of the wretched pityful creatures of this World; nay would make them *Eat your Book*, which you have made as bitter a pill for them as possible.

LORD BATHURST ON SWIFT

Bathurst's letter to Swift, 9 Sept. 1730

YOU have taken all the precautions wch a prudent man cou'd possibly, to break off an impertinent correspondence, & yet it won't doe. One must be more stupid than a Dutch Burgur Master not to see thro' the design of the last letter—*I show* 30 *all yr letters to our Irish Wits—One of them is going to write a treatise of English Bulls & Blunders*—and for further security yu add at last *I'm going to take a Progress God knows where & shall be back again God knows when.* I have given yu a reasonable breathing time and now I must att yu again. I receive so much Pleasure in reading yr letters that according to the usuall Good nature & justice of Mankind I can dispense with the trouble I give yu in reading mine. But if yu grow obstinate & won't answer me I'll plague yu & Pester yu & doe all I can to Vex yu I'll take yr works to Peices & show yu that it is all borrow'd or stoln, have not yu stoln the sweetness of yr Numbers from Dryden & Waller, have not yu borrow'd thoughts from Virgil & Horace, at least I am sure I have seen something like them in those Books, & in yr Prose writings, wch they make such a Noise abt, they are only some little improvements upon the Humour yu have stoln from Miguel de Cervantes & Rabelais. well but the Stile—a great matter indeed for an English man to value himself upon, that he can write English. why I write English too, but 'tis in another stile.

But I won't forget yr Political tracts yu may say that yu have ventur'd yr Ears at one time & yr Neck at another for the Good of the Country, why that other People have done in another manner upon less occasions and are not at all Proud of it. you have overturn'd & supported Ministers yu have sett Kingdoms in a Flame by yr Pen. Pray wt is there in that, but having the Nack of hitting the Passions of Mankind, with that alone, & a little knowledge of Ancient & Modern History, & seeing a little further into the inside of things than the Generality of Men, yu have made this bustle. there is no Wit in any of them, I have read them all over & don't remember any of those pretty flowers those just antitheses, wch one meets with so frequently in the French writers. none of those clever turns upon words nor those apt quotations out of Latin Authors wch the writers of the last Age amongst us abounded in. None of those pretty similes wch some of our Modern Authors adorn their works with that are not only a little like the things they wou'd illustrate but are also like twenty other things. In short as often as I have read any of y^{r} tracts I have been so tir'd with them that I have never been easy till I got to the End of them. I have found my brain heated my Imagination fir'd just as if I was drunk. a Pretty thing indeed for one of y^{r} Gown to value Himself upon, that with sitting still an hour in his study he has often made three Kingdoms drunk at once.

I have twenty other points to maul y^{u} upon if y^{u} provoke me but if y^{u} are civil & Good natur'd & will send me a long, a very long letter in answer to this I will lett y^{u} alone a good while Well Adieu now if I had had a better Pen I can tell y^{u} that I shou'd not have concluded so soon.

LORD ORRERY ON SWIFT

From Orrery's *Remarks*, 1752, 2nd ed.

IF we consider his prose works, we shall find a certain masterly conciseness in their style, that has never been equalled by any other writer. The truth of this assertion will more evidently appear, by comparing him with some of the authors of his own time. Of these Dr. Tillotson, and Mr. Addison, are to be numbered among the most eminent. Addison has all the powers that can captivate and improve: his diction is easy, his periods are well turned, his expressions are flowing, and his humour is delicate. Tillotson is nervous, grave, majestic, and perspicuous. We must join both these characters together to form a true idea of Dr. Swift: yet as he outdoes Addison in humour, he excels Tillotson in perspicuity. The Archbishop indeed confined himself to subjects relative to his profession: but Addison and Swift are more diffusive writers. They continually vary in their manner, and treat different topics in a different style. When the

writings of Addison terminate in party, he loses himself extremely, and from a delicate, and just comedian, deviates into one of the lowest kind. Not so Dr. Swift; he appears like a masterly gladiator. He wields the sword of party with ease, justness and dexterity: and while he entertains the ignorant and the vulgar, he draws an equal attention from the learned and the great. When he is serious, his gravity becomes him. When he laughs, his readers must laugh with him. But, what shall be said for his love of trifles, and his
10 want of delicacy and decorum? Errors, that if he did not contract, at least he encreased in *Ireland*. They are without a parallel. I hope they will ever remain so. The first of them, arose meerly from his love of flattery, with which he was daily fed in that kingdom: the second, proceeded from the misanthropy of his disposition, which induced him peevishly to debase mankind, and even to ridicule human nature itself. Politics were his favourite topic, as they gave him an opportunity of gratifying his ambition, and thirst of power: yet even in this road, he has seldom continued long in one par-
20 ticular path. He has written miscellaneously, and has chosen rather to appear a wandering comet, than a fixed star. Had he applied the faculties of his mind to one great, and useful work, he must have shined more gloriously, and might have enlightened a whole planetary system in the political world.

The poetical performances of Dr. Swift ought to be considered as occasional poems written either to please, or vex some particular persons. We must not suppose them designed for posterity: if he had cultivated his genius in that
30 way, he must certainly have excelled, especially in satyr. We see fine sketches, in several of his pieces; but he seems more desirous to inform, and strengthen his mind, than to indulge the luxuriancy of his imagination. He chooses to discover, and correct errors in the works of others, rather than to illustrate, and add beauties to his own. Like a skilful

artist, he is fond of probing wounds to their depth, and of enlarging them to open view. He prefers caustics, which erode proud flesh, to softer balsamics, which give more immediate ease. He aims to be severely useful, rather than politely engaging: and as he was either not formed, or would not take pains to excel in poetry, he became, in some measure, superior to it; and assumed more the air and manners of a critic, than of a poet.

DR. DELANY ON SWIFT

From Delany's *Observations*, 1754

My Lord, when you consider Swift's singular, peculiar, and most variegated vein of wit, always rightly intended (al- 10 though not always so rightly directed), delightful in many instances, and salutary, even where it is most offensive; when you consider his strict truth, his fortitude in resisting oppression and arbitrary power; his fidelity in friendship, his sincere love and zeal for religion, his uprightness in making right resolutions, and his steadiness in adhering to them; his care of his church, its choir, its œconomy, and its income; his attention to all those that preached in his cathedral, in order to their amendment in pronunciation and style; as also his remarkable attention to the interest of his successors, 20 preferably to his own present emoluments; [his] invincible patriotism, even to a country which he did not love; his very various, well-devised, well-judged, and extensive charities, throughout his life, and his whole fortune (to say nothing of his wife's) conveyed to the same Christian purposes at his death—charities from which he could enjoy no honour, advantage or satisfaction of any kind in this world. When you consider his ironical and humorous, as well as his serious schemes, for the promotion of true religion and virtue; his success in soliciting for the First Fruits and Twentieths, to 30 the unspeakable benefit of the established Church of Ireland;

and his felicity (to rate it no higher) in giving occasion to the building of fifty new churches in London.

All this considered, the character of his life will appear like that of his writings; they will both bear to be re-considered and re-examined with the utmost attention, and always discover new beauties and excellences upon every examination.

They will bear to be considered as the sun, in which the brightness will hide the blemishes; and whenever petulant 10 ignorance, pride, malice, malignity, or envy interposes to cloud or sully his fame, I will take upon me to pronounce that the eclipse will not last long.

To conclude—no man ever deserved better of any country than Swift did of his. A steady, persevering, inflexible friend; a wise, a watchful, and a faithful counsellor, under many severe trials and bitter persecutions, to the manifest hazard both of his liberty and fortune.

He lived a blessing, he died a benefactor, and his name will ever live an honour to Ireland.

DR. JOHNSON ON SWIFT

From Johnson's *Life of Swift*, 1781

20 WHEN Swift is considered as an author it is just to estimate his powers by their effects. In the reign of Queen Anne he turned the stream of popularity against the Whigs, and must be confessed to have dictated for a time the political opinions of the English nation. In the succeeding reign he delivered Ireland from plunder and oppression, and shewed that wit, confederated with truth, had such force as authority was unable to resist. He said truly of himself that Ireland 'was his debtor'. It was from the time when he first began to patronize the Irish that they may date their riches and 30 prosperity. He taught them first to know their own interest, their weight, and their strength, and gave them spirit to

assert that equality with their fellow-subjects to which they have ever since been making vigorous advances, and to claim those rights which they have at last established. Nor can they be charged with ingratitude to their benefactor, for they reverenced him as a guardian and obeyed him as a dictator.

In his works he has given very different specimens, both of sentiment and expression. His *Tale of a Tub* has little resemblance to his other pieces. It exhibits a vehemence and rapidity of mind, a copiousness of images, and vivacity of 10 diction such as he afterwards never possessed or never exerted. It is of a mode so distinct and peculiar that it must be considered by itself; what is true of that is not true of any thing else which he has written.

In his other works is found an equable tenour of easy language, which rather trickles than flows. His delight was in simplicity. That he has in his works no metaphor, as has been said, is not true; but his few metaphors seem to be received rather by necessity than choice. He studied purity; and though perhaps all his structures are not exact, yet it 20 is not often that solecisms can be found: and whoever depends on his authority may generally conclude himself safe. His sentences are never too much dilated or contracted; and it will not be easy to find any embarrassment in the complication of his clauses, any inconsequence in his connections, or abruptness in his transitions.

His style was well suited to his thoughts, which are never subtilised by nice disquisitions, decorated by sparkling conceits, elevated by ambitious sentences, or variegated by far-sought learning. He pays no court to the passions; he 30 excites neither surprise nor admiration; he always understands himself, and his reader always understands him: the peruser of Swift wants little previous knowledge; it will be sufficient that he is acquainted with common words and common things; he is neither required to mount elevations nor to explore profundities; his passage is always on a level, along solid ground, without asperities, without obstruction.

This easy and safe conveyance of meaning it was Swift's desire to attain, and for having attained he deserves praise, though perhaps not the highest praise. For purposes merely didactick, when something is to be told that was not known before, it is the best mode, but against that inattention by which known truths are suffered to lie neglected it makes no provision; it instructs, but does not persuade.

SIR WALTER SCOTT ON SWIFT

From Scott's *Life of Swift*, 1814

10 As an Author, there are three peculiarities remarkable in the character of Swift. The first of these has been rarely conceded to an author, at least by his contemporaries. It is the distinguished attribute of originality, and it cannot be refused to Swift by the most severe critic. Even Johnson has allowed that perhaps no author can be found who has borrowed so little, or has so well maintained his claim to be considered as original. There was indeed nothing written before his time which could serve for his model, and the few hints which he has adopted from other authors bear no more 20 resemblance to his compositions than the green flax to the cable which is formed from it.

The second peculiarity, which has indeed been already noticed, is his total indifference to literary fame. Swift executed his various and numerous works as a carpenter forms wedges, mallets, or other implements of his art, not with the purpose of distinguishing himself by the workmanship bestowed on the tools themselves, but solely in order to render them fit for accomplishing a certain purpose, beyond which they were of no value in his eyes. He is often anxious about 30 the success of his argument, and angrily jealous of those who debate the principles and the purpose for which he assumes the pen, but he evinces, on all occasions, an unaffected indifference for the fate of his writings, providing the end of their publication was answered. The careless mode in which Swift suffered his works to get to the public, his refusing them the credit of his name, and his renouncing all connection with the profits of literature, indicate his disdain of the character of a professional author.

The third distinguishing mark of Swift's literary character is, that, with the exception of history, (for his fugitive attempts in Pindaric and Latin verse are too unimportant 10 to be noticed,) he has never attempted any stile of composition in which he has not obtained a distinguished pitch of excellence. We may often think the immediate mode of exercising his talents trifling, and sometimes coarse and offensive; but his Anglo-latin verses, his riddles, his indelicate descriptions, and his violent political satires, are in their various departments as excellent as the subjects admitted, and only leave us room occasionally to regret that so much talent was not uniformly employed upon nobler topics. 20

As a poet Swift's post is pre-eminent in the sort of poetry which he cultivated. He never attempted any species of composition, in which either the sublime or the pathetic were required of him. But in every department of poetry where wit is necessary, he displayed, as the subject chanced to require, either the blasting lightning of satire, or the lambent and meteor-like coruscations of frolicsome humour. His powers of versification are admirably adapted to his favourite subjects. Rhyme, which is a handcuff to an inferior poet, he who is master of his art wears as a bracelet. 30 Swift was of the latter description; his lines fall as easily into the best grammatical arrangement, and the most simple and forcible expression, as if he had been writing in prose. The numbers and the coincidence of rhymes, always correct and natural, though often unexpected, distinguish the current of his poetical composition, which exhibits, otherwise, no mark of the difficulty with which these graces are attained. In respect of matter, Swift seldom elevates his tone above a satirical diatribe, a moral lesson, or a poem on manners; but the former are unrivalled in severity, and the latter in ease. Sometimes, however, the intensity of his satire gives to his poetry a character of emphatic violence, which borders upon grandeur. This is peculiarly distinguishable in the Rhapsody on Poetry. Yet this grandeur is founded, not 10 on sublimity either of conception or expression, but upon the energy of both; and indicates rather ardour of temper, than power of imagination. *Facit indignatio versus.* The elevation of tone arises from the strong mood of passion rather than from poetical fancy.

WILLIAM HAZLITT ON SWIFT

From Hazlitt's *Lectures on the English Poets,* 1818

SWIFT'S reputation as a poet has been in a manner obscured by the greater splendour, by the natural force and inventive genius of his prose writings; but if he had never written either the *Tale of a Tub* or *Gulliver's Travels,* his name merely as a poet would have come down to us, and 20 have gone down to posterity with well-earned honours. His Imitations of Horace, and still more his Verses on his own Death, place him in the first rank of agreeable moralists in verse. There is not only a dry humour, an exquisite tone of irony, in these productions of his pen; but there is a touching, unpretending pathos, mixed up with the most whimsical and eccentric strokes of pleasantry and satire. His Description of the Morning in London, and of a City Shower, which were first published in *The Tatler,* are among the most delightful of the contents of that very delightful work. Swift 30 shone as one of the most sensible of the poets; he is also distinguished as one of the most nonsensical of them. No man has written so many lack-a-daisical, slip-shod, tedious, trifling, foolish, fantastical verses as he, which are so little an imputation on the wisdom of the writer; and which, in fact, only shew his readiness to oblige others, and to forget himself. He has gone so far as to invent a new stanza of fourteen and sixteen syllable lines for Mary the cookmaid to vent her budget of nothings, and for Mrs. Harris to gossip with the deaf old housekeeper. Oh, when shall we have such another Rector of Laracor!—*The Tale of a Tub* is one of the most masterly compositions in the language, whether for 10 thought, wit, or style. It is so capital and undeniable a proof of the author's talents, that Dr. Johnson, who did not like Swift, would not allow that he wrote it. It is hard that the same performance should stand in the way of a man's promotion to a bishopric, as wanting gravity, and at the same time be denied to be his, as having too much wit. It is a pity the Doctor did not find out some graver author, for whom he felt a critical kindness, on whom to father this splendid but unacknowledged production. Dr. Johnson could not deny that *Gulliver's Travels* were his; he therefore disputed their 20 merits, and said that after the first idea of them was conceived, they were easy to execute; all the rest followed mechanically. I do not know how that may be; but the mechanism employed is something very different from any that the author of Rasselas was in the habit of bringing to bear on such occasions. There is nothing more futile, as well as invidious, than this mode of criticising a work of original genius. Its greatest merit is supposed to be in the invention; and you say, very wisely, that it is not *in the execution*. You might as well take away the merit of the invention of the 30 telescope, by saying that, after its uses were explained and understood, any ordinary eyesight could look through it. Whether the excellence of *Gulliver's Travels* is in the conception or the execution, is of little consequence; the power is somewhere, and it is a power that has moved the world.

The power is not that of big words and vaunting common places. Swift left these to those who wanted them; and has done what his acuteness and intensity of mind alone could enable any one to conceive or to perform. His object was to strip empty pride and grandeur of the imposing air which external circumstances throw around them; and for this purpose he has cheated the imagination of the illusions which the prejudices of sense and of the world put upon it, by reducing every thing to the abstract predicament of size. He enlarges or diminishes the scale, as he wishes to shew the insignificance or the grossness of our over-weening self-love. That he has done this with mathematical precision, with complete presence of mind and perfect keeping, in a manner that comes equally home to the understanding of the man and of the child, does not take away from the merit of the work or the genius of the author. He has taken a new view of human nature, such as a being of a higher sphere might take of it; he has torn the scales from off his moral vision; he has tried an experiment upon human life, and sifted its pretensions from the alloy of circumstances; he has measured it with a rule, has weighed it in a balance, and found it, for the most part, wanting and worthless—in substance and in shew. Nothing solid, nothing valuable is left in his system but virtue and wisdom. What a libel is this upon mankind! What a convincing proof of misanthropy! What presumption and what *malice prepense*, to shew men what they are, and to teach them what they ought to be! What a mortifying stroke aimed at national glory, is that unlucky incident of Gulliver's wading across the channel and carrying off the whole fleet of Blefuscu! After that, we have only to consider which of the contending parties was in the right. What a shock to personal vanity is given in the account of Gulliver's nurse Glumdalclitch! Still, notwithstanding the disparagement to her personal charms, her good-nature remains the same amiable quality as before. I cannot see the harm, the misanthropy, the immoral and degrading tendency of this. The moral lesson is as fine as the intellectual exhibition is amusing. It is an attempt to tear off the mask of imposture from the world; and nothing but imposture has a right to complain of it. It is, indeed, the way with our quacks in morality to preach up the dignity of human nature, to pamper pride and hypocrisy with the idle mockeries of the virtues they pretend to, and which they have not: but it was not Swift's way to cant morality, or any thing else; nor did his genius prompt him to write unmeaning panegyrics on mankind! 10

I do not, therefore, agree with the estimate of Swift's moral or intellectual character, given by an eminent critic, who does not seem to have forgotten the party politics of Swift. I do not carry my political resentments so far back: I can at this time of day forgive Swift for having been a Tory. I feel little disturbance (whatever I might think of them) at his political sentiments, which died with him, considering how much else he has left behind him of a more solid and imperishable nature! If he had, indeed (like some others), merely left behind him the lasting infamy of a destroyer of his country, or the shining example of 20 an apostate from liberty, I might have thought the case altered.

The determination with which Swift persisted in a preconcerted theory, savoured of the morbid affection of which he died. There is nothing more likely to drive a man mad, than the being unable to get rid of the idea of the distinction between right and wrong, and an obstinate, constitutional preference of the true to the agreeable. Swift was not a Frenchman. In this respect he differed from Rabelais and Voltaire. They have been accounted the three greatest wits in modern times; but their wit was of a peculiar kind in each. 30 They are little beholden to each other; there is some resemblance between Lord Peter in the *Tale of a Tub*, and Rabelais' Friar John; but in general they are all three authors of a substantive character in themselves. Swift's wit (particularly in his chief prose works) was serious,

saturnine, and practical; Rabelais' was fantastical and joyous; Voltaire's was light, sportive, and verbal. Swift's wit was the wit of sense; Rabelais', the wit of nonsense; Voltaire's, of indifference to both. The ludicrous in Swift arises out of his keen sense of impropriety, his soreness and impatience of the least absurdity. He separates, with a severe and caustic air, truth from falsehood, folly from wisdom, 'shews vice her own image, scorn her own feature', and it is the force, the precision, and the honest abruptness with
10 which the separation is made, that excites our surprise, our admiration, and laughter. He sets a mark of reprobation on that which offends good sense and good manners, which cannot be mistaken, and which holds it up to our ridicule and contempt ever after. His occasional disposition to trifling (already noticed) was a relaxation from the excessive earnestness of his mind. *Indignatio facit versus.* His better genius was his spleen. It was the biting acrimony of his temper that sharpened his other faculties. The truth of his perceptions produced the pointed coruscations of his wit; his
20 playful irony was the result of inward bitterness of thought; his imagination was the product of the literal, dry, incorrigible tenaciousness of his understanding. He endeavoured to escape from the persecution of realities into the regions of fancy, and invented his Lilliputians and Brobdingnagians, Yahoos, and Houyhnhnms, as a diversion to the more painful knowledge of the world around him: *they* only made him laugh, while men and women made him angry. His feverish impatience made him view the infirmities of that great baby the world, with the same scrutinizing glance and jealous
30 irritability that a parent regards the failings of its offspring; but, as Rousseau has well observed, parents have not on this account been supposed to have more affection for other people's children than their own. In other respects, and except from the sparkling effervescence of his gall, Swift's brain was as 'dry as the remainder biscuit after a voyage'.

D. NICHOL SMITH ON SWIFT'S READING

From the Introduction to *A Tale of a Tub*, 1920

SWIFT liked to think of the difficulties his readers would find in the *Tale*. He too was a 'mysterious writer', quite as mysterious as any of the writers he satirized. 'It were much to be wisht', he says, 'and I do here humbly propose for an Experiment, that every Prince in *Christendom* will take seven of the *deepest Scholars* in his Dominions, and shut them up close for *seven* Years, in *seven* Chambers, with a Command to write *seven* ample Commentaries on this comprehensive discourse. I shall venture to affirm, that whatever Difference may be found in their several Conjectures, they will be all, without the least Distortion, manifestly deduceable from the Text.' Some of the deductions were more serious for him than he had suspected; they barred his way to high office in the Church, and they induced him to write an Apology. But in the glow of composition he found new zest in imagining his readers wondering what he could mean. He would have been pleased had he heard Bishop Burnet declaring that for his part he could find out neither head nor tail. To us nowadays the main drift of the book is clear and unmistakable. It is a satire on the abuses in religion, with satires on the abuses in learning introduced by way of digressions. After two centuries of annotation it still has its puzzles in plenty. In not a few passages the more knowing readers in Swift's own day may have found the meaning and purpose that we miss. But the wealth of detailed allusion must always have been baffling; and Swift meant it to be so. 'I believe one of the Author's Designs', he makes his annotator say, 'was to set curious Men a hunting thro' Indexes, and enquiring for Books out of the common Road.' He issued a solemn warning to 'those whom the *Learned* among Posterity will appoint for Commentators upon this elaborate Treatise'; and they dare never forget that he may be playing a game with them. The modern editor must always be conscious of the shade of Swift finding amused pleasure in the false surmises that send him searching on the wrong track, and when the hunt is successful, as often by luck as by skill, in the explanations that sometimes come perilously near pedantry.

Swift's reading was remarkably wide. In his younger days he was a hard student, and he had the use of a good library 10 when he lived with Sir William Temple at Moor Park. During the third and most important period of his residence there, from May 1696 till Temple's death in January 1699, he employed his leisured independence in varied and constant study. The *Tale* was written, mainly if not wholly, at this time. He wrote it from a full mind. He speaks humorously of his 'indefatigable reading'. The humour of the passage cannot conceal its sober truth.

His references to his commonplace-books are likewise not to be dismissed as mere satire. He finds, he says, that his 20 commonplace-book fills much slower than he had reason to expect; he has 'a laborious Collection of Seven Hundred Thirty Eight *Flowers*, and *shining Hints* of the best *Modern* Authors', digested with great reading into a book of common-places; he lays his memorandums before him and inserts them 'with a wonderful facility of application'. The satire here is so obvious that we are apt to see nothing but satire. Moreover, these passages are of a piece with many others in the *Tale*. One of its many recurring themes is that learning is abused by excessive reliance on commonplace- 30 books, as on indexes, epitomes, and other devices that save the trouble of reading and thinking. He never spares the 'judicious Collectors of *bright Parts*, and *Flowers*, and *Observanda's*'. What though the head be empty, he asks, provided the commonplace-book be full? We may therefore not suspect how assiduous he was in making abstracts of the authors that he read. The real difference between him and the 'judicious collectors' was that his head and his commonplace-book were both full at the same time. Deane Swift and Hawkesworth tell us that copious extracts from Cyprian, Irenaeus, Sleidan's Commentaries, and Sarpi's history of the Council of Trent were found among his papers, and that they appeared from memorandums in his own writing to have been made while he lived with Temple. To this list Dr. John Lyon added Tertullian, Epiphanius, Diodorus Siculus, and Thucydides. Swift had his own commonplace-books, and epitomes, and abstracts. He made them in the process of filling and exercising his mind, about the very time when he was engaged on the *Tale*.

Fortunately we have a list of books read by Swift in 1697 and at the beginning of 1698, apparently one of the memorandums to which Deane Swift and Hawkesworth refer. It survives in a transcript made by John Lyon, and bound in at the beginning of Lyon's annotated copy of Hawkesworth's *Life of Swift*:

While he was at *Moor park*, he kept an Acct one Year of the Books he read in the following manner—

From Jan: 7. 169$\frac{6}{7}$.

Lord Herbert's Harry 8. fol
Sleidan's Com̄ent: abstracted fol
Council of *Trent* abstr: fol
Virgil, bis
Horace, 9. volumes
Sr *W. Temple*'s Memoirs
—— Introduction
Camden's *Elisabeth*
Prince *Arthur*
Histoire de *Chypre*
Voyage de *Syam*
Voiture
Memoires de *Maurier*
Lucius Florus, ter

Collier's Essays 2 volumes
Count *Gabalis*
Sr *John Davis* of the Soul
Conformité de Religion, &c
Dialogues de Morts, 2 Vol:
Lucretius, ter
Histoire de Mr *Constance*
Histoire d'*Æthiopie*
Historie de *Cotes* de &c
10 *Diodorus Siculus,* abstr: f^{o}
Cyprian & *Irenæus* abstr: f^{o}
Voyage de *Maroc* &c
Ælian, 1st Vol:
Homer, Iliad & Odyss.
Cicero's Epistles
Bernier's Grand Mogol 2 Vol:
Burnet's Hist: of Reform: f^{o}
Petronius Arbiter
Oevres Melées 5 Vol:

20 From Jan: 7th 169$\frac{7}{8}$

Thucydides by *Hobbes* f^{ol} abstracted
Theophrasti Characteres.
Vossius de Sybillinis

No farther Acc^{t} remains of his Studys at this time.

This list contains two of the small number of modern books that Swift cited in his marginal notes, the *Histoire de M. Constance* by the Père d'Orléans, and Bernier's *Grand Mogol.* Neither of the citations can be dated before the middle of 1697. About the same time he read the passage 30 from Irenæus that he gave on his title-page. The quotations from Lucretius must likewise have been suggested by his three recent readings. Other books on the list supplied him with allusions. He appears, for instance, sometimes to have remembered Jeremy Collier's *Essays upon Several Moral Subjects*; he certainly remembered Blackmore's *Prince Arthur*. The annotator who had the energy to work his way through all the books in Swift's list would probably be able to overburden his notes with a large number of parallel passages. But the list has a much wider interest. It admits us, as it were, to a secret view of Swift's habits of mind when he was gaining his full powers, and Swift never wrote anything that gives a greater sense of sheer power than some of the later sections of the *Tale*.

The list gives only a fraction of the reading that went to the making of the *Tale*. His constant allusions to the classics are drawn from a very large number of authors, not merely 10 from the authors that he read in 1697, but even from Pausanias, Photius, and Hippocrates. His knowledge of rosicrucian and alchemical literature ranged far beyond the *Comte de Gabalis*; he had found prolonged amusement in the 'dark authors', and notably in Paracelsus and Thomas Vaughan. As a churchman he knew the Fathers, and the controversial literature of the seventeenth century. In the household of Temple he was familiar with every detail of the controversy on the letters of Phalaris, and the wider controversy on the Ancients and Moderns. He could speak 20 with authority on current criticism and the productions of Grub Street. He was equally at home in Rabelais and Cervantes. And already he had long been preparing himself for *Gulliver's Travels*. The list includes accounts of travels and descriptions of far-away countries such as the *Voyage de Syam*, the *Histoire d'Æthiopie*, and the *Voyage de Maroc*, and they are among its most interesting entries. The *Tale* itself shows that he knew Heylyn's *Cosmography*, Guagninus's *Sarmatiae Descriptio*, and Hall's *Mundus Alter et Idem*. 30

All this multifarious reading is placed under contribution. At one time it is Hippocrates or the Schoolmen, Bentley or Scaliger, Cervantes or the Apocrypha; at another Dick Whittington and his Cat somehow get into the same sentence with Jehuda Hannasi and the Jerusalem Mishna. Yet the *Tale* remains one of the most original books ever written. 'The author's wit was entirely his own.' The ingredients of a dozen *Tales* lie ready to hand for any writer who has the wit to make another. Though the book is a tissue of allusions, Swift could well insist upon it, that throughout it all he had not borrowed one single hint from any writer in the world. Many years afterwards he made the same proud boast in his verses 'On the Death of Dr. Swift':

> To steal a hint was never known,
> But what he writ was all his own.

Two other books must be mentioned, both of which Swift knew much better than might be suspected. The first is Sir Thomas Browne's *Vulgar Errors*. It appears to have suggested not only the use of some uncommon words like 'exantlation', 'atramentous', and 'fuliginous', but also the passages about the orientation of man's body, the description of Moses, the white powder that kills without report, the belief that by slitting the ear of a stag the defect may be spread through a whole herd, and the story of the Macrocephali. Swift might have been directly indebted to the same sources as Browne, but, taken together, these points of contact are satisfactory evidence that the *Vulgar Errors* was one of his favourite volumes. The other book is Marvell's *Rehearsal Transpros'd*. There he met with the whale and the tub and could learn that a straight line if continued far enough could become a circle. He also found the familiar story about the same food appearing again and again at table in different guises. In Italian it is 'tutta fava'; in French 'toujours perdrix'. Swift has 'it is all *Pork*', and cites Plutarch in the margin. He might also have cited Marvell. He refers to the *Rehearsal Transpros'd* in his 'Apology' as a book that we still read 'with pleasure'. The style of Swift is Swift himself, a style which has never been imitated successfully, and could not be formed by imitation. But when we read Marvell after reading Swift we feel the kinship in the muscular strength, the simplicity that is fraught with meaning, and the seemingly careless ease that comes from perfect confidence.

THE DRAPIER'S LETTERS and *GULLIVER'S TRAVELS*

From the Introduction to *The Letters of Jonathan Swift to Charles Ford*, 1935

We learn one or two new points about *The Drapier's Letters*. Swift's earliest reference to Wood's coinage in all his correspondence was made to Ford on 13 February 1724, when he says 'I can not tell whether I shall see you in the Spring, for I am afraid our Farthings will not pass in'. He says nothing as yet about the role of Drapier, but he must 10 have assumed it about this time, as when he next wrote to Ford, on 2 April, he speaks of his first *Letter* as being widely circulated throughout Ireland:

> I do not know whether I told you that I sent out a small Pamphlet under the Name of a Draper, laying the whole Vilany open, and advising People what to do; about 2000 of them have been dispersd by Gentlemen in severall Parts of the Country.

The *Letter* must thus have been published as 'a pamphlet' by the middle of March, and it was probably written in the latter half of February. Another brief statement shows Swift 20 in touch with the Grand Juries who protected the printer:

> The grand Jury has been dissolved for refusing to present a Paper against Wood [i.e. *Seasonable Advice to the Grand Jury*]; a Second was called who are more stubborn.

This was written on the day before the second Grand Jury took the bold course of making a presentment not against the printer but against Wood and his patent. A minor point of interest is the spelling of 'Drapier'. The name occurs eight times in these letters to Ford, and the first four times it is spelled 'Draper', and afterwards a fifth time; 'Drapier' occurs only thrice, and not till four of the *Letters* had been published. Swift was not a stickler for spelling, but we are left wondering whether 'Drapier' was his own choice for his title pages, or whether it was the fancy of the printer.

But there is nothing of greater interest in these letters than the new and conclusive information which they supply about *Gulliver's Travels*. The date of composition was long a problem. Delany, who had the means of knowing but was
10 careless, said confidently that the book was not written until some years after 1720. Orrery and Deane Swift said equally confidently that it was written between 1714 and 1720; and two allusions in letters sent to Swift seemed to lend some support to this earlier date. When Bolingbroke said in his letter of 1 January 1722 'I long to see your Travels', he might have implied that the book was finished; and when Vanessa in her letter of June 1722 showed that she was familiar with an episode in the Voyage to Brobdingnag, she might be taken to have read the book in manu-
20 script. So long as the evidence was of this kind, and so long as the evidence provided in plenty by the subject-matter of the book was neglected, the view generally held was that *Gulliver's Travels* was completed by 1720, as if it was the product of the six years of depression when Swift was settling down for life in Ireland, and as if, for reasons which were never explained, it should then have been kept for six years unprinted. Swift had given no help in his correspondence. Though Bolingbroke and Vanessa might allude to *Gulliver's Travels*, he himself had never once mentioned it
30 in any known letter.

He had mentioned it in his letters to Ford, to whom he also spoke about it when they met in Ireland. What he wrote about it—all that he is known to have written about it while he was engaged on it—is here set down together with the dates:

15 April 1721.—I am now writing a History of my Travells, which will be a large Volume, and gives Account of Countryes hitherto unknown; but they go on slowly for want of Health and Humor.

22 July 1722 (Lough-Gall).—The bad Weather has made me read through abundance of Trash, and this hath made me almost forget how to hold a Pen, which I must therefore keep for Dublin, Winter and Sickness.

19 January 1724.—I was at a Loss about one of the Letters, at first, but after found it was to you, and that you are a Traytor into the Bargain: else how should he [Bolingbroke] know any Thing of Stella or of Horses. Tis hard that Folks in France will not let us in Ireland be quiet. I would have him and you know that I hate Yahoos of both Sexes, and that Stella and Madame de Villette are onely tolerable at best, for want of Houyhnhnms.

— My greatest want here is of somebody qualifyed to censure and correct what I write, I know not above two or three whose Judgment I would value, and they are lazy, negligent, and without any Opinion of my Abilityes. I have left the Country of Horses, and am in the flying Island, where I shall not stay long, and my two last Journyes will be soon over.

13 February 1724.—He [Bolingbroke] raillyes me upon my Southern Journey, says, and swears it is no Pun, That Stella fixed my Course, talks of the Houyhnhnms as if he were acquainted with them, and in that shows you as a most finished Traitor, for which you make very indifferent Excuses.

2 April 1724.—I shall have finished my Travells very soon if I have Health, Leisure, and humor.

14 August 1725 (Quilca).—I have finished my Travells, and I am now transcribing them; they are admirable Things, and will wonderfully mend the World.

16 August 1725 (Quilca).—I am amusing my self in the Quality of Bayliff to Sheridan, among Bogs and Rocks, overseeing and ranting at Irish Laborers, reading Books twice over for want of fresh ones, and fairly correcting and transcribing my Travells, for the Publick.

From these passages it is now clear that Swift was at work in earnest in 1721, that he had written the draft of the first

two Voyages before the end of 1723, that he wrote the fourth Voyage next and had completed the draft by January 1724, and that he was then engaged on the third Voyage. At the beginning of April he expected to finish the book 'very soon'. But in February or March he had begun *The Drapier's Letters,* and he was occupied with them till the end of the year. The revision of the *Travels* and the incorporation of new material, suggested partly by the circumstances which had called forth the *Letters,* may be assigned to 1725. By
10 August of that year he had finished his *Travels* and was transcribing them.

'Simplicity without which no human performance can arrive to any great perfection'—these are his own words. The simplicity of his style did not come by chance. He had long thought of a satire in the form of travels, but once he had found his design he did not write in haste. He was engaged on *Gulliver's Travels* for four years. He wrote it in draft, then he made additions and corrections, and then a fair copy. Revision was an important stage in the process
20 of composition.

Much of the revision, and possibly most of it, was done at Quilca in County Cavan, the country 'cabin' of Thomas Sheridan, to which he retired with Stella and Mrs. Dingley towards the end of April 1725, with the hope—we may assume—of a clear stretch for undisturbed writing. It was as bad a summer as he had known. 'I can do no work this terrible weather, which has put us all seventy times out of patience', he wrote to Sheridan in June. But he found 'some agreeablenesses' in the wild country, and his health was
30 better than it had been in Dublin. There is a rising note of cheerfulness in the letters which he wrote at this time, but to nobody, not even to his absent host, did he mention *Gulliver* before he told Ford that he had finished it. His nearest approach to mentioning it is in a letter to Pope where he speaks of grand designs that are all in prose. To

others he would say that when he could not stir out because of the weather he was reading some easy trash merely to divert himself; he even asked Sheridan to send him a large bundle of school exercises, good as well as bad, to correct. Possibly no one except Stella knew how busily he was passing his time in that wild country and that bad summer. In his last letter to Ford, in March, he had spoken of the Drapier and not of Gulliver. He had his recurring fits of deafness, but he completed the task which he had set himself, and his spirits were high when, with the frankness which he seems to have reserved for Ford, he announced on finishing his *Travels* that 'they are admirable things and will wonderfully mend the world'.

The little that Swift's friends in England knew about *Gulliver* while it was being written, they learned from Ford. Swift roundly declares him a traitor for telling Bolingbroke about the Houyhnhnms, but bore him no ill will. The Houyhnhnms and the Yahoos were, in the main, the work of 1723, the year in which Stella paid her long visit to Woodpark, and Ford must have divulged the secret on his return to England at the end of the year. That Bolingbroke regarded it as a secret is shown by his discreet silence in the letter which he wrote to Swift on the same day as he wrote to Ford rather foolishly about the Dean and Stella and horses. Even his statement in January 1722 'I long to see your Travels' may be explained by a hint from Ford that the book was begun. Likewise when Pope said in September 1725 'your Travels I hear much of', he had heard of them from Ford; and then in reply Swift, for the first time, wrote openly to Pope about them, in the well-known letter in which he speaks of his hatred of that animal called man and his love of John, Peter, and Thomas. The secret appears to have been well kept in Ireland. Sheridan in September 1725 could understand an allusion to the Yahoos. But there is no evidence that any one ever saw the manuscript except

Ford; and there is none that he saw it till it was finished, unless Swift's complaint that he has no one qualified to censure and correct what he writes be taken to imply that Ford had performed that service when in Ireland.

Note

This is the last volume in the Clarendon Series which the late General Editor, Professor D. Nichol Smith, proposed. I undertook to prepare it shortly before his death. It has therefore not received the benefit of his supervision; and I doubt whether he would have allowed me to quote so fully from his own writings. But it has seemed to me appropriate now to place here his comments on Swift's best works; for he has thrown fresh light on his methods of composition and the qualities of his mind. H. D.

Selections from

JONATHAN SWIFT'S POETRY AND PROSE

Satire

From *The Battle of the Books: The Preface of the Author*

SATYR *is a sort of* Glass, *wherein Beholders do generally discover every body's Face but their Own; which is the chief Reason for that kind of Reception it meets in the World, and that so very few are offended with it. But if it should happen otherwise, the Danger is not great; and, I have learned from long Experience, never to apprehend Mischief from those Understandings, I have been able to provoke; For, Anger and Fury, though they add Strength to the* Sinews *of the* Body, *yet are found to relax those of the* Mind, *and to render all its Efforts*
10 *feeble and impotent.*

There is a Brain *that will endure but one* Scumming: *Let the Owner gather it with Discretion, and manage his little Stock with Husbandry; but of all things, let him beware of bringing it under the* Lash *of his* Betters; *because, That will make it all bubble up into Impertinence, and he will find no new Supply: Wit, without knowledge, being a Sort of* Cream, *which gathers in a Night to the Top, and by a skilful Hand, may be soon* whipt *into* Froth; *but once scumm'd away, what appears underneath will be fit for nothing, but to be thrown to*
20 *the Hogs.*

The Spider and the Bee

From *The Battle of the Books*, 1704

THINGS were at this Crisis, when a material Accident fell out. For, upon the highest Corner of a large Window, there dwelt a certain *Spider*, swollen up to the first Magnitude, by the Destruction of infinite Numbers of *Flies*, whose Spoils lay scattered before the Gates of his Palace, like human Bones before the Cave of some Giant. The Avenues to his Castle were guarded with Turn-pikes, and Palissadoes, after all the *Modern* way of Fortification. After you had passed several Courts, you came to the Center, wherein you might behold the *Constable* himself in his own Lodgings, which had Windows fronting to each Avenue, and Ports to sally out upon all Occasions of Prey or Defence. In this Mansion he had for some Time dwelt in Peace and Plenty, without Danger to his *Person* by *Swallows* from above, or to his *Palace* by *Brooms* from below: When it was the Pleasure of Fortune to conduct thither a wandring *Bee,* to whose Curiosity a broken Pane in the Glass had discovered it self; 10 and in he went, where expatiating a while, he at last happened to alight upon one of the outward Walls of the *Spider's* Cittadel; which yielding to the unequal Weight, sunk down to the very Foundation. Thrice he endeavoured to force his Passage, and Thrice the Center shook. The *Spider* within, feeling the terrible Convulsion, supposed at first, that *Nature* was approaching to her final Dissolution; or else, that *Beelzebub* with all his Legions, was come to revenge the Death of many thousands of his Subjects, whom this Enemy had slain and devoured. However, he at length valiantly resolved 20 to issue forth, and meet his Fate. Mean while, the *Bee* had acquitted himself of his Toils, and posted securely at some Distance, was employed in cleansing his Wings, and disengaging them from the ragged Remnants of the Cobweb. By this time the *Spider* was adventured out, when beholding the Chasms, and Ruins, and Dilapidations of his Fortress, he was very near at his Wit's end, he stormed and swore like a Mad-man, and swelled till he was ready to burst. At length, casting his Eye upon the *Bee,* and wisely gathering Causes from Events, (for they knew each other by Sight) 30 *A Plague split you,* said he, *for a giddy Son of a Whore; Is it you, with a Vengeance, that have made this Litter here? Could you not look before you, and be d———n'd? Do you think I have nothing else to do (in the Devil's Name) but to Mend and Repair after your Arse? Good Words, Friend,* said

the *Bee,* (having now pruned himself, and being disposed
to drole) *I'll give you my Hand and Word to come near your
Kennel no more; I was never in such a confounded Pickle since
I was born. Sirrah,* replied the *Spider, if it were not for breaking an old Custom in our Family, never to stir abroad against
an Enemy, I should come and teach you better Manners. I pray,
have Patience,* said the *Bee, or you will spend your Substance,
and for ought I see, you may stand in need of it all, towards the
Repair of your House. Rogue, Rogue,* replied the *Spider, yet,*
10 *methinks, you should have more Respect to a Person, whom all
the World allows to be so much your Betters. By my Troth,* said
the *Bee, the Comparison will amount to a very good Jest, and
you will do me a Favour, to let me know the Reasons, that all
the World is pleased to use in so hopeful a Dispute.* At this,
the *Spider* having swelled himself into the Size and Posture
of a Disputant, began his Argument in the true Spirit of
Controversy, with a Resolution to be heartily scurrilous and
angry, to urge *on* his own Reasons, without the least Regard
to the Answers or Objections of his Opposite; and fully
20 predetermined in his Mind against all Conviction.

Not to disparage my self, said he, *by the Comparison with
such a Rascal; What art thou but a Vagabond without House
or Home, without Stock or Inheritance; Born to no Possession of your own, but a Pair of Wings, and a Drone-Pipe.
Your Livelihood is an universal Plunder upon Nature;
a Freebooter over Fields and Gardens; and for the sake of
Stealing, will rob a Nettle as readily as a Violet. Whereas I am
a domestick Animal, furnisht with a Native Stock within my
self. This large Castle* (*to shew my Improvements in the*
30 *Mathematicks*) *is all built with my own Hands, and the
Materials extracted altogether out of my own Person.*

I am glad, answered the *Bee, to hear you grant at least, that
I am come honestly by my Wings and my Voice, for then, it
seems, I am obliged to Heaven alone for my Flights and my
Musick; and Providence would never have bestowed on me two*

such Gifts, without designing them for the noblest Ends. I visit, indeed, all the Flowers and Blossoms of the Field and the Garden, but whatever I collect from thence, enriches my self, without the least Injury to their Beauty, their Smell, or their Taste. Now, for you and your Skill in Architecture, and other Mathematicks, I have little to say: In that Building of yours, there might, for ought I know, have been Labor and Method enough, but by woful Experience for us both, 'tis too plain, the Materials are nought, and I hope, you will henceforth take Warning, and consider Duration and matter, as well as method and Art. You boast, indeed, of being obliged to no other Creature, but of drawing, and spinning out all from your self; That is to say, if we may judge of the Liquor in the Vessel by what issues out, You possess a good plentiful Store of Dirt and Poison in your Breast; And, tho' I would by no means, lessen or disparage your genuine Stock of either, yet, I doubt you are somewhat obliged for an Encrease of both, to a little foreign Assistance. Your inherent Portion of Dirt, does not fail of Acquisitions, by Sweepings exhaled from below: and one Insect furnishes you with a share of Poison to destroy another. So that in short the Question comes all to this; Whether is the nobler Being of the two, That which by a lazy Contemplation of four Inches round; by an over-weening Pride, which feeding and engendering on it self, turns all into Excrement and Venom; producing nothing at last, but Flybane and a Cobweb: Or That, which, by an universal Range, with long Search, much Study, true Judgment, and Distinction of Things, brings home Honey and Wax.

This Dispute was managed with such Eagerness, Clamor, and Warmth, that the two Parties of *Books* in Arms below, stood Silent a while, waiting in Suspense what would be the Issue; which was not long undetermined: For the *Bee* grown impatient at so much loss of Time, fled strait away to a bed of Roses, without looking for a Reply; and left the *Spider* like an Orator, *collected* in himself, and just prepared to burst out.

It happened upon this Emergency, that *Æsop* broke silence first. He had been of late most barbarously treated by a strange Effect of the *Regent's Humanity,* who had tore off his Title-page, sorely defaced one half of his Leaves, and chained him fast among a Shelf of *Moderns.* Where soon discovering how high the Quarrel was like to proceed, He tried all his Arts, and turned himself to a thousand Forms: At length in the borrowed Shape of an *Ass,* the *Regent* mistook him for a *Modern*; by which means, he had Time and Opportunity to escape to the *Antients,* just when the *Spider* and the *Bee* were entring into their Contest; to which He gave His Attention with a world of Pleasure; and when it was ended, swore in the loudest Key, that in all his Life, he had never known two Cases so parallel and adapt to each other, as That in the Window, and this upon the Shelves. The *Disputants,* said he, *have admirably managed the Dispute between them, have taken in the full Strength of all that is to be said on both sides, and exhausted the Substance of every Argument* pro *and* con. *It is but to adjust the Reasonings of both to the present Quarrel, then to compare and apply the Labors and Fruits of each, as the* Bee *has learnedly deduced them; and we shall find the Conclusion fall plain and close upon the* Moderns *and* Us. *For, pray Gentlemen, was ever any thing so* Modern *as the* Spider *in his Air, his Turns, and his Paradoxes? He argues in the Behalf of* You *his Brethren, and Himself, with many Boastings of his native Stock, and great Genius; that he Spins and Spits wholly from himself, and scorns to own any Obligation or Assistance from without. Then he displays to you his great Skill in Architecture, and Improvement in the Mathematicks. To all this, the* Bee, *as an Advocate, retained by us the* Antients, *thinks fit to Answer; That if one may judge of the great Genius or Inventions of the* Moderns, *by what they have produced, you will hardly have Countenance to bear you out in boasting of either. Erect your Schemes with as much Method and Skill as you please; yet, if the materials be nothing but Dirt, spun out of your own Entrails, (the Guts of* Modern *Brains) the Edifice will conclude at last in a* Cobweb: *The Duration of which, like that of other* Spiders *Webs, may be imputed to their being forgotten, or neglected, or hid in a Corner. For any Thing else of Genuine, that the* Moderns *may pretend to, I cannot recollect; unless it be a large Vein of Wrangling and Satyr, much of a Nature and Substance with the* Spider's *Poison; which, however, they pretend to spit wholly out of themselves, is improved by the same Arts, by feeding upon the* Insects *and* Vermin *of the Age. As for* Us, *the* Antients, 10 *We are content with the* Bee, *to pretend to Nothing of our own, beyond our* Wings *and our* Voice: *that is to say, our* Flights *and our* Language; *For the rest, whatever we have got, has been by infinite Labor, and search, and ranging thro' every Corner of Nature: The Difference is, that instead of* Dirt *and* Poison, *we have rather chose to fill our Hives with* Honey *and* Wax, *thus furnishing Mankind with the two Noblest of Things, which are* Sweetness *and* Light.

A Digression on Madness

From *A Tale of a Tub,* sect. ix, 1704

HAVING therefore so narrowly past thro' this intricate Difficulty, the Reader will, I am sure, agree with me in the 20 Conclusion; that if the *Moderns* mean by *Madness,* only a Disturbance or Transposition of the Brain, by Force of certain *Vapours* issuing up from the lower Faculties; Then has this *Madness* been the Parent of all those mighty Revolutions, that have happened in *Empire,* in *Philosophy,* and in *Religion.* For, the Brain, in its natural Position and State of Serenity, disposeth its Owner to pass his Life in the common Forms, without any Thought of subduing Multitudes to his own *Power,* his *Reasons* or his *Visions*; and the more he shapes his Understanding by the Pattern of Human 30

Learning, the less he is inclined to form Parties after his particular Notions; because that instructs him in his private Infirmities, as well as in the stubborn Ignorance of the People. But when a Man's Fancy gets *astride* on his Reason, when Imagination is at Cuffs with the Senses, and common Understanding, as well as common Sense, is Kickt out of Doors; the first Proselyte he makes, is Himself, and when that is once compass'd, the Difficulty is not so great in bringing over others; A strong Delusion always operating
10 from *without*, as vigorously as from *within*. For, Cant and Vision are to the Ear and the Eye, the same that Tickling is to the Touch. Those Entertainments and Pleasures we most value in Life, are such as *Dupe* and play the Wag with the Senses. For, if we take an Examination of what is generally understood by *Happiness*, as it has Respect, either to the Understanding or the Senses, we shall find all its Properties and Adjuncts will herd under this short Definition: That, *it is a perpetual Possession of being well Deceived*. And first, with Relation to the Mind or Understanding; 'tis
20 manifest, what mighty Advantages Fiction has over Truth; and the Reason is just at our Elbow; because Imagination can build nobler Scenes, and produce more wonderful Revolutions than Fortune or Nature will be at Expence to furnish. Nor is Mankind so much to blame in his Choice, thus determining him, if we consider that the Debate meerly lies between *Things past*, and *Things conceived*; and so the Question is only this; Whether Things that have Place in the *Imagination*, may not as properly be said to *Exist*, as those that are seated in the *Memory*; which may be justly
30 held in the Affirmitive, and very much to the Advantage of the former, since This is acknowledged to be the *Womb* of Things, and the other allowed to be no more than the *Grave*. Again, if we take this Definition of Happiness, and examine it with Reference to the Senses, it will be acknowledged wonderfully adapt. How fade and insipid do all Objects

accost us that are not convey'd in the Vehicle of *Delusion?* How shrunk is every Thing, as it appears in the Glass of Nature? So, that if it were not for the Assistance of Artificial *Mediums,* false Lights, refracted Angles, Varnish, and Tinsel; there would be a mighty Level in the Felicity and Enjoyments of Mortal Men. If this were seriously considered by the World, as I have a certain Reason to suspect it hardly will; Men would no longer reckon among their high Points of Wisdom, the Art of exposing weak Sides, and publishing Infirmities; an Employment in my Opinion, neither better 10 nor worse than that of *Unmasking,* which I think, has never been allowed fair Usage, either in the *World* or the *Play-House.*

In the Proportion that Credulity is a more peaceful Possession of the Mind, than Curiosity, so far preferable is that Wisdom, which converses about the Surface, to that pretended Philosophy which enters into the Depth of Things, and then comes gravely back with Informations and Discoveries, that in the inside they are good for nothing. The two Senses, to which all Objects first address themselves, 20 are the Sight and the Touch; These never examine farther than the Colour, the Shape, the Size, and whatever other Qualities dwell, or are drawn by Art upon the Outward of Bodies; and then comes Reason officiously, with Tools for cutting, and opening, and mangling, and piercing, offering to demonstrate, that they are not of the same consistence quite thro'. Now, I take all this to be the last Degree of perverting Nature: one of whose Eternal Laws it is, to put her best Furniture forward. And therefore, in order to save the Charges of all such expensive Anatomy for the Time to 30 come; I do here think fit to inform the Reader, that in such Conclusions as these, Reason is certainly in the Right; and that in most Corporeal Beings, which have fallen under my Cognizance, the *Outside* hath been infinitely preferable to the *In:* Whereof I have been farther convinced from some

late Experiments. Last Week I saw a Woman *flay'd,* and you will hardly believe, how much it altered her Person for the worse. Yesterday I ordered the Carcass of a *Beau* to be stript in my Presence; when we were all amazed to find so many unsuspected Faults under one Suit of Cloaths: Then I laid open his *Brain,* his *Heart,* and his *Spleen;* But, I plainly perceived at every Operation, that the farther we proceeded, we found the Defects encrease upon us in Number and Bulk: from all which, I justly formed this Con-
10 clusion to my self; That whatever Philosopher or Projector can find out at Art to sodder and patch up the Flaws and Imperfections of Nature, will deserve much better of Mankind, and teach us a more useful Science, than that so much in present Esteem, of widening and exposing them (like him who held *Anatomy* to be the ultimate End of *Physick.*) And he, whose Fortunes and Dispositions have placed him in a convenient Station to enjoy the Fruits of this noble Art; He that can with *Epicurus* content his Ideas with the *Films* and *Images* that fly off upon his Senses from the *Superficies*
20 of Things; Such a Man truly wise, creams off Nature, leaving the Sower and the Dregs, for Philosophy and Reason to lap up. This is the sublime and refined Point of Felicity, called, *the Possession of being well deceived*; The Serene Peaceful State of being a Fool among Knaves.

But to return to *Madness.* It is certain, that according to the System I have above deduced; every *Species* thereof proceeds from a Redundancy of *Vapour;* therefore, as some Kinds of *Phrenzy* give double Strength to the Sinews, so there are of other *Species,* which add Vigor and Life, and
30 Spirit to the Brain: Now, it usually happens, that these active Spirits, getting Possession of the Brain, resemble those that haunt other waste and empty Dwellings, which for want of Business, either vanish, and carry away a Piece of the House, or else stay at home and fling it all out of the Windows. By which are mystically display'd the two

principal Branches of *Madness*, and which some Philosophers not considering so well as I, have mistook to be different in their Causes, over-hastily assigning the first to Deficiency, and the other to Redundance.

I think it therefore manifest, from what I have here advanced, that the main Point of Skill and Address, is to furnish Employment for this Redundancy of *Vapour*, and prudently to adjust the Seasons of it; by which means it may certainly become of Cardinal and Catholick Emolument in a Commonwealth. Thus one Man chusing a proper 10 Juncture, leaps into a Gulph, from thence proceeds a Hero, and is called the Saver of his Country; Another atchieves the same Enterprise, but unluckily timing it, has left the Brand of *Madness*, fixt as a Reproach upon his Memory; Upon so nice a Distinction are we taught to repeat the Name of *Curtius* with Reverence and Love; that of *Empedocles*, with Hatred and Contempt. Thus, also it is usually conceived, that the Elder *Brutus* only personated the *Fool* and *Madman*, for the Good of the Publick: but this was nothing else, than a Redundancy of the same *Vapor*, long misapplied, 20 called by the *Latins*, *Ingenium par negotiis*: Or, (to translate it as nearly as I can) a sort of *Phrenzy*, never in its right Element, till you take it up in Business of the State.

Upon all which, and many other Reasons of equal Weight, though not equally curious; I do here gladly embrace an Opportunity I have long sought for, of Recommending it as a very noble Undertaking, to Sir *E——d S——r*, Sir *C——r M——ve*, Sir *J——n B——ls*, *J——n H——w*, Esq; and other Patriots concerned, that they would move for Leave to bring in a Bill, for appointing Commissioners to Inspect 30 into *Bedlam*, and the Parts adjacent; who shall be empowered to *send for Persons, Papers, and Records:* to examine into the Merits and Qualifications of every Student and Professor; to observe with utmost Exactness their several Dispositions and Behaviour; by which means, duly distinguishing and adapting their Talents, they might produce admirable Instruments for the several Offices in a State, *Civil* and *Military*; proceeding in such methods as I shall here humbly propose. And, I hope the Gentle Reader will give some Allowance to my great Solicitudes in this important Affair, upon Account of that high Esteem I have ever born that honourable Society, whereof I had some Time the Happiness to be an unworthy Member.

Is any Student tearing his Straw in piece-meal, Swearing 10 and Blaspheming, biting his Grate, foaming at the Mouth, and emptying his Pispot in the Spectator's Faces? Let the Right Worshipful, the *Commissioners of Inspection*, give him a Regiment of Dragoons, and send him into *Flanders* among the *Rest*. Is another eternally talking, sputtering, gaping, bawling, in a Sound without Period or Article? What wonderful Talents are here mislaid! Let him be furnished immediately with a green Bag and Papers, and [1]*three Pence* in his Pocket, and away with Him to *Westminster-Hall*. You will find a Third, gravely taking the Dimensions of his 20 Kennel; A Person of Foresight and Insight, tho' kept quite in the Dark; for why, like *Moses*, *Ecce* [2]*cornuta erat ejus facies*. He walks duly in one Pace, intreats your Penny with due Gravity and Ceremony; talks much of hard Times, and Taxes, and the *Whore of Babylon*; Bars up the woodden Window of his Cell constantly at eight a Clock: Dreams of *Fire*, and *Shop-lifters*, and *Court-Customers*, and *Priviledg'd* Places. Now, what a Figure would all these Acquirements amount to, if the Owner were sent into the *City* among his Brethren! Behold a Fourth, in much and deep Conversation 30 with himself, biting his Thumbs at proper Junctures; His Countenance chequered with Business and Design; sometimes walking very fast, with his Eyes nailed to a Paper

[1] *A Lawyer's Coach-hire.*

[2] Cornutus, *is either Horned or Shining, and by this Term,* Moses *is described in the vulgar* Latin *of the Bible.*

that he holds in his Hands: A great Saver of Time, somewhat thick of Hearing, very short of Sight, but more of Memory. A Man ever in Haste, a great Hatcher and Breeder of Business, and excellent at the Famous Art of *whispering Nothing*. A huge Idolater of Monosyllables and Procrastination; so ready to *Give* his Word to every Body, that he never *keeps* it. One that has forgot the common *Meaning* of Words, but an admirable Retainer of the *Sound*. Extreamly subject to the *Loosness*, for his *Occasions* are perpetually *calling him away*. If you approach his Grate in his familiar 10 Intervals; *Sir*, says he, *Give me a Penny, and I'll sing you a Song: But give me the Penny first*. (Hence comes the common Saying, and commoner Practice of parting with Money for a *Song*.) What a compleat System of *Court-Skill* is here described in every Branch of it, and all utterly lost with wrong Application? Accost the Hole of another Kennel, first stopping your Nose, you will behold a surley, gloomy, nasty, slovenly Mortal, raking in his own Dung, and dabling in his Urine. The best Part of his Diet, is the Reversion of his own Ordure, which exspiring into Steams, whirls per- 20 petually about, and at last reinfunds. His Complexion is of a dirty Yellow, with a thin scattered Beard, exactly agreeable to that of his Dyet upon its first Declination; like other Insects, who having their Birth and Education in an Excrement, from thence borrow their Colour and their Smell. The Student of this Apartment is very sparing in his Words, but somewhat over-liberal of his Breath; He holds his Hand out ready to receive your Penny, and immediately upon Receipt, withdraws to his former Occupations. Now, is it not amazing to think, the Society of *Warwick-Lane*, should have 30 no more Concern, for the Recovery of so useful a Member, who, if one may judge from these Appearances, would become the greatest Ornament to that Illustrious Body? Another Student struts up fiercely to your Teeth, puffing with his Lips, half squeezing out his Eyes, and very graciously holds you out his Hand to kiss. The *Keeper* desires you not to be afraid of this Professor, for he will do you no Hurt: To him alone is allowed the Liberty of the Anti-Chamber, and the *Orator* of the Place gives you to understand, that this solemn Person is a *Taylor* run mad with Pride. This considerable Student is adorned with many other Qualities, upon which, at present, I shall not farther enlarge. — — [1]*Heark in your Ear* — — — — — — — I am strangely mistaken, if all his Address, his Motions, and his Airs, 10 would not then be very natural, and in their proper Element.

I shall not descend so minutely, as to insist upon the vast Number of *Beaux, Fidlers, Poets,* and *Politicians,* that the World might recover by such a Reformation; But what is more material, besides the clear Gain redounding to the Commonwealth, by so large an Acquisition of Persons to employ, whose Talents and Acquirements, if I may be so bold to affirm it, are now buried, or at least misapplied: It would be a mighty Advantage accruing to the Publick from this Enquiry, that all these would very much excel, and 20 arrive at great Perfection in their several Kinds; which, I think, is manifest from what I have already shewn; and shall inforce by this one plain Instance; That even, I my self, the Author of these momentous Truths, am a Person, Whose Imaginations are hard-mouth'd, and exceedingly disposed to run away with his *Reason,* which I have observed from long Experience, to be a very light Rider, and easily shook off; upon which Account, my Friends will never trust me alone, without a solemn Promise, to vent my Speculations in this, or the like manner, for the universal Benefit of Human kind; 30 which, perhaps, the gentle, courteous, and candid Reader, brimful of that *Modern* Charity and Tenderness, usually annexed to his *Office,* will be very hardly persuaded to believe.

[1] *I cannot conjecture what the Author means here, or how this Chasm could be fill'd, tho' it is capable of more than one Interpretation.*

A Meditation upon a Broom-stick

Written August 1704, first published in *Miscellanies*, 1711

THIS single Stick, which you now behold ingloriously lying in that neglected Corner, I once knew in a flourishing State in a Forest: It was full of Sap, full of Leaves, and full of Boughs: But now, in vain does the busy Art of Man pretend to vye with Nature, by tying that withered Bundle of Twigs to its sapless Trunk: It is now at best but the Reverse of what it was; a Tree turned upside down, the Branches on the Earth, and the Root in the Air: It is now handled by every dirty Wench, condemned to do her Drudgery; and, 10 by a capricious kind of Fate, destined to make other Things Clean, and be Nasty itself. At length, worn to the Stumps in the Service of the Maids, it is either thrown out of Doors, or condemned to the last Use of kindling a Fire. When I beheld this, I sighed, and said within my self, SURELY MORTAL MAN IS A BROOM-STICK; Nature sent him into the World strong and lusty in a thriving Condition, wearing his own Hair on his Head, the proper Branches of this Reasoning Vegetable; till the Axe of Intemperance has lopp'd off his green Boughs, and left him a withered Trunk: 20 He then flies to Art, and puts on a Periwig; valuing himself upon an unnatural Bundle of Hairs, all covered with Powder that never grew on his Head; but now should this our Broom-stick pretend to enter the Scene, proud of those Birchen Spoils it never bore, and all covered with Dust, though the Sweepings of the finest Lady's Chamber; we should be apt to ridicule and despise its Vanity. Partial Judges that we are of our own Excellencies, and other Men's Defaults!

But a Broom-stick, perhaps you will say, is an Emblem of 30 a Tree standing on its Head; and pray what is Man, but a topsy-turvy Creature, his Animal Faculties perpetually mounted on his Rational; his Head where his Heels should be, groveling on the Earth! And yet, with all his Faults, he sets up to be an universal Reformer and Corrector of Abuses; a Remover of Grievances; rakes into every Slut's Corner of Nature, bringing hidden Corruptions to the Light, and raises a mighty Dust where there was none before; sharing deeply all the while in the very same Pollutions he pretends to sweep away. His last Days are spent in Slavery to Women, and generally the least deserving; till worn to the Stumps, like his Brother Bezom, he is either kicked out of Doors, or 10 made use of to kindle Flames, for others to warm themselves by.

An Argument against Abolishing Christianity

Written 1708, first published in *Miscellanies*, 1711

An Argument to prove, that the abolishing of Christianity in England, May, as Things now Stand, be attended with some Inconveniencies, and perhaps, not produce those many good Effects proposed thereby.

I AM very sensible what a Weakness and Presumption it is, to reason against the general Humour and Disposition of the World. I remember it was with great Justice, and a due Regard to the Freedom both of the Publick and the Press, forbidden upon several Penalties to write, or discourse, or 20 lay wagers against the Union even before it was confirmed by Parliament: because that was looked upon as a Design to oppose the Current of the People, which besides the Folly of it, is a manifest Breach of the fundamental Law, that makes this Majority of Opinion the Voice of God. In like manner, and for the very same reasons, it may perhaps be neither safe nor prudent to argue against the abolishing of Christianity, at a Juncture when all Parties seem so unanimously determined upon the Point; as we cannot but allow from their Actions, their Discourses, and their Writings. 30 However, I know not how, whether from the Affectation of Singularity, or the Perverseness of human Nature; but so it unhappily falls out, that I cannot be entirely of this Opinion. Nay, although I were sure an Order were issued out for my immediate Prosecution by the Attorney-General; I should still confess, that in the present Posture of our Affairs at home or abroad, I do not yet see the absolute Necessity of extirpating the Christian Religion from among us.

This perhaps may appear too great a Paradox even for our wise and paradoxical Age to endure; therefore I shall handle it with all Tenderness, and with the utmost Deference to that great and profound Majority which is of another Sentiment.

And yet the Curious may please to observe, how much the Genius of a Nation is liable to alter in half an Age: I have heard it affirmed for certain by some very old People, that the contrary Opinion was even in their Memories as much in vogue as the other is now; and that a Project for the abolishing of Christianity would then have appeared as singular, and been thought as absurd, as it would be at this Time to write or discourse in its Defence.

Therefore I freely own, that all Appearances are against me. The System of the Gospel, after the Fate of other Systems, is generally antiquated and exploded; and the Mass or Body of the common People, among whom it seems to have had its latest Credit, are now grown as much ashamed of it as their Betters: Opinions, like Fashions, always, descending from those of Quality to the middle Sort, and thence to the Vulgar, where at length they are dropped and vanish.

But here I would not be mistaken, and must therefore be so bold as to borrow a Distinction from the Writers on the other Side, when they make a Difference betwixt nominal and real Trinitarians. I hope no Reader imagines me so weak to stand up in the Defence of *real* Christianity, such as used in primitive Times (if we may believe the Authors of those Ages) to have an Influence upon Men's Belief and Actions:

To offer at the restoring of that, would indeed be a wild Project, it would be to dig up Foundations; to destroy at one Blow *all* the Wit, and *half* the Learning of the Kingdom; to break the entire Frame and Constitution of Things; to ruin Trade, extinguish Arts and Sciences, with the Professors of them; in short, to turn our Courts, Exchanges, and Shops into Desarts; and would be full as absurd as the Proposal of Horace, where he advises the Romans, all in a Body, to leave their City and seek a new Seat in some re-
10 mote Part of the World, by way of a Cure for the Corruption of their Manners.

Therefore I think this Caution was in itself altogether unnecessary, (which I have inserted only to prevent all possibility of Cavilling) since every candid Reader will easily understand my Discourse to be intended only in Defence of *nominal* Christianity, the other having been for some time wholly laid aside by general Consent, as utterly inconsistent with all our present Schemes of Wealth and Power.

Another Advantage proposed by the abolishing of Christi-
20 anity, is the clear Gain of one Day in seven, which is now entirely lost, and consequently the Kingdom one seventh less considerable in Trade, Business, and Pleasure; beside the Loss to the Publick of so many stately Structures now in the Hands of the Clergy; which might be converted into Play-houses, Exchanges, Market-houses, common Dormitories, and other publick Edifices.

I hope I shall be forgiven a hard Word if I call this a perfect Cavil. I readily own there hath been an old Custom, Time out of mind, for People to assemble in the Churches
30 every Sunday, and that Shops are still frequently shut, in order, as it is conceived, to preserve the Memory of that ancient Practice; but how this can prove a Hindrance to Business or Pleasure, is hard to imagine. What if the Men of Pleasure are forced, one Day in the Week, to game at Home, instead of the Chocolate-House? Are not the

Taverns and Coffee-Houses open? Can there be a more convenient Season for taking a Dose of Physick? Are fewer Claps got upon Sundays than other Days? Is not that the chief Day for Traders to sum up the Accounts of the Week, and for Lawyers to prepare their Briefs? But I would fain know how it can be pretended that the Churches are misapplied. Where are more Appointments and Rendezvouzes of Gallantry? Where more Care to appear in the foremost Box with greater Advantage of Dress? Where more Meetings for Business? Where more Bargains driven of all Sorts? 10
and where so many Conveniencies or Incitements to Sleep?

And therefore, if notwithstanding all I have said, it still be thought necessary to have a Bill brought in for repealing Christianity, I would humbly offer an Amendment, That instead of the Word *Christianity,* may be put *Religion* in general; which I conceive will much better answer all the good Ends proposed by the Projectors of it. For, as long as we leave in being a God, and his Providence, with all the necessary Consequences which curious and inquisitive Men will be apt to draw from such Premises, we do not strike at 20
the Root of the Evil, though we should ever so effectually annihilate the present Scheme of the Gospel. For, of what Use is Freedom of Thought, if it will not produce Freedom of Action; which is the sole End, how remote soever in Appearance, of all Objections against Christianity? And therefore, the Free-Thinkers consider it as a Sort of Edifice, wherein all the Parts have such a mutual Dependance on each other, that if you happen to pull out one single Nail, the whole Fabrick must fall to the Ground. This was happily expressed by him who had heard of a Text brought for 30
proof of the Trinity, which in an ancient Manuscript was differently read; he thereupon immediately took the Hint, and by a sudden Deduction of a long Sorites, most Logically concluded: Why, if it be as you say, I may safely whore and drink on, and defy the Parson, From which, and many the

like Instances easy to be produced, I think nothing can be more manifest, than that the Quarrel is not against any particular Points of hard Digestion in the Christian System, but against Religion in general, which, by laying Restraints on human Nature, is supposed the great Enemy to the Freedom of Thought and Action.

Upon the whole, if it shall still be thought for the Benefit of Church and State, that Christianity be abolished, I conceive however, it may be more convenient to defer the Execution to a Time of Peace, and not venture in this Conjuncture to disoblige our Allies; who, as it falls out, are all Christians, and many of them, by the Prejudices of their Education, so bigotted, as to place a sort of Pride in the Appellation. If upon being rejected by them, we are to trust to an Alliance with the Turk, we shall find our selves much deceived: For, as he is too remote, and generally engaged in War with the Persian Emperor, so his People would be more scandalized at our Infidelity, than our Christian Neighbours. Because, the Turks are not only strict Observers of religious Worship, but, what is worse, believe a God; which is more than is required of us, even while we preserve the Name of Christians.

To conclude: Whatever some may think of the great Advantages to Trade by this favourite Scheme, I do very much apprehend, that in six Months Time after the Act is past for the Extirpation of the Gospel, the Bank and East-India Stock, may fall at least One per Cent. And, since that is fifty Times more than ever the Wisdom of our Age thought fit to venture for the *Preservation* of Christianity, there is no Reason we should be at so great a Loss, merely for the sake of *destroying* it.

A Letter to a Young Gentleman lately entered into Holy Orders, (1720)

I COULD likewise have been glad if you had applied your self a little more to the Study of the English Language, than I fear you have done; the Neglect whereof is one of the most general Defects among the Scholars of this Kingdom, who seem to have not the least Conception of a Style, but run on in a flat kind of Phraseology, often mingled with barbarous Terms and Expressions, peculiar to the Nation: Neither do I perceive that any Person, either finds or acknowledges his Wants upon this Head, or in the least desires to have them supplied. Proper Words in proper 10 Places, makes the true Definition of a Style. But this would require too ample a Disquisition to be now dwelt on: However, I shall venture to name one or two Faults, which are easy to be remedied with a very small Portion of Abilities.

The first is the frequent Use of obscure Terms, which by the Women are called *hard Words*, and by the better sort of Vulgar *fine Language*; than which I do not know a more universal, inexcusable, and unnecessary Mistake among the Clergy of all Distinctions, but especially the younger Practitioners. I have been curious enough to take a List of 20 several hundred Words in a Sermon of a new Beginner, which not one of his Hearers, among a hundred, could possibly understand; neither can I easily call to mind any Clergyman of my own Acquaintance who is wholly exempt from this Error; although many of them agree with me in the Dislike of the Thing. But I am apt to put my self in the Place of the Vulgar, and think many Words difficult or obscure, which they will not allow to be so, because those Words are obvious to Scholars. I believe the Method observed by the famous Lord Falkland, in some of his Writings, 30 would not be an ill one for young Divines: I was assured by an old Person of Quality who knew him well, that when he

doubted whether a Word were perfectly intelligible, or no, he used to consult one of his Lady's Chambermaids, (not the Waiting-woman, because it was possible she might be conversant in Romances,) and by her Judgment was guided, whether to receive, or to reject it. And if that great Person thought such a Caution necessary in Treatises offered to the learned World, it will be sure, at least as proper in Sermons, where the meanest Hearer is supposed to be concerned, and where very often a Lady's Chambermaid may be allowed to
10 equal half the Congregation, both as to Quality and Understanding. But I know not how it comes to pass, that Professors in most Arts and Sciences are generally the worst qualified to explain their Meanings to those who are not of their Tribe: A common Farmer shall make you understand in three Words, that his Foot is out of Joint, or his Collarbone broken; wherein a Surgeon, after a hundred Terms of Art, if you are not a Scholar, shall leave you to seek. It is frequently the same Case in Law, Physick, and even many of the meaner Arts.

20 It would be endless to run over the several Defects of Style among us: I shall therefore say nothing of the Mean and the Paultry, (which are usually attended by the Fustian,) much less of the Slovenly or Indecent. Two Things I will just warn you against: The First is, the Frequency of flat, unnecessary Epithets; and the other is, the Folly of using old thread-bare Phrases, which will often make you go out of your Way to find and apply them; are nauseous to rational Hearers, and will seldom express your Meaning as well as your own natural Words.

30 Although, as I have already observed, our English Tongue is too little cultivated in this Kingdom, yet the Faults are Nine in Ten owing to Affectation, and not to the Want of Understanding. When a Man's Thoughts are clear, the properest Words will generally offer themselves first; and his own Judgment will direct him in what Order to

place them, so as they may be best understood. Where Men err against this Method, it is usually on purpose, and to shew their Learning, their Oratory, their Politeness, or their Knowledge of the World. In short, that Simplicity, without which no human Performance can arrive to any great Perfection, is no where more eminently useful than in this.

If a rational Man reads an excellent Author with just Application, he shall find himself extreamly improved, and perhaps insensibly led to imitate that Author's Perfections, although in a little Time he should not remember one Word 10 in the Book, nor even the Subject it handled: For Books give the same Turn to our Thoughts and Way of Reasoning, that good and ill Company does to our Behaviour and Conversation; without either loading our Memories, or making us even sensible of the Change. And particularly I have observed in Preaching, that no Men succeed better than those, who trust entirely to the Stock or Fund of their own Reason, advanced indeed, but not overlaid by Commerce with Books. Whoever only reads in order to transcribe wise and shining Remarks, without entering into the Genius and 20 Spirit of the Author, as it is probable he will make no very judicious Extract, so he will be apt to trust to that Collection in all his Compositions, and be misled out of the regular Way of Thinking, in order to introduce those Materials which he has been at the Pains to gather: And the Product of all this will be found a manifest incoherent Piece of Patchwork.

Some Gentlemen abounding in their University Erudition, are apt to fill their Sermons with Philosophical Terms and Notions of the metaphysical or abstracted Kind; which 30 generally have one Advantage, to be equally understood by the Wise, the Vulgar, and the Preacher himself. I have been better entertained, and more informed by a Chapter in the *Pilgrim's Progress*, than by a long Discourse upon the Will and the Intellect, and simple or complex Ideas. Others again, are fond of dilating on Matter and Motion, talk of the fortuitous Concourse of Atoms, of Theories, and Phæno-mena; directly against the Advice of St. Paul, who yet appears to have been conversant enough in those kinds of Studies.

I do not find that you are any where directed in the Canons or Articles, to attempt explaining the Mysteries of the Christian Religion. And indeed, since Providence in-tended there should be Mysteries, I do not see how it can be agreeable to Piety, Orthodoxy, or good Sense, to go about such a Work. For, to me there seems to be a manifest Dilemma in the Case: If you explain them, they are Mys-teries no longer; if you fail, you have laboured to no Pur-pose. What I should think most reasonable and safe for you to do upon this Occasion, is upon solemn Days to deliver the Doctrine as the Church holds it, and confirm it by Scrip-ture. For my part, having considered the Matter impartially, I can see no great Reason which those Gentlemen, you call the Free-Thinkers, can have for their Clamour against religious Mysteries; since it is plain, they were not invented by the Clergy, to whom they bring no Profit, nor acquire any Honour. For every Clergyman is ready, either to tell us the utmost he knows, or to confess that he does not under-stand them: neither is it strange that there should be Mysteries in Divinity, as well as in the commonest Opera-tions of Nature.

A Letter to a Young Lady on her Marriage

First published in *Miscellanies*, Vol. 1, 1727

Madam,

THE hurry and impertinence of receiving and paying Visits on account of your Marriage, being now over, you are beginning to enter into a Course of Life, where you will want much Advice to divert you from falling into many Errors, Fopperies, and Follies to which your Sex is subject. I have always borne an entire Friendship to your Father and Mother; and the Person they have chosen for your Husband, hath been for some Years past my particular Favourite. I have long wished you might come together, because I hoped, that from the goodness of your Disposition, and by following the Council of wise Friends, you might in time make your self worthy of him. Your Parents were so far in the right, that they did not produce you much into the World; whereby you avoided many wrong Steps which others have taken; and have fewer ill Impressions to be removed: But they failed, as it is generally the Case, in too much neglecting to cultivate your Mind; without which it is impossible to acquire or preserve the Friendship and Esteem of a Wise Man, who soon grows weary of acting the Lover and treating his Wife like a Mistress, but wants a reasonable Companion, and a true Friend through every Stage of his Life. It must be therefore your Business to qualify your self for those Offices; wherein I will not fail to be your Director as long as I shall think you deserve it, by letting you know how you are to act, and what you ought to avoid.

And beware of despising or neglecting my Instructions, whereon will depend, not only your making a good figure in the World, but your own real Happiness, as well as that of the Person who ought to be the Dearest to you.

I must therefore desire you in the first place to be very slow in changing the modest behaviour of a Virgin: It is usual in young wives before they have been many Weeks married, to assume a bold, forward Look and manner of Talking; as if they intended to signify in all Companies, that they were no longer Girls, and consequently that their whole Demeanor, before they got a Husband, was all but a Countenance and Constraint upon their Nature: Whereas,

I suppose, if the Votes of wise Men were gathered, a very great Majority would be in favour of those Ladies, who after they were entered into that State, rather chose to double their portion of Modesty and Reservedness.

I must likewise warn you strictly against the least degree of Fondness to your Husband before any Witnesses whatsoever, even before your nearest Relations, or the very Maids of your Chamber. This proceeding is so exceeding odious and disgustful to all who have either good Breeding or good
10 Sense, that they assign two very unamiable Reasons for it; the one is gross Hypocrisy, and the other has too bad a Name to mention. If there is any difference to be made, your Husband is the lowest Person in Company, either at Home or Abroad; and every Gentleman present hath a better claim to all marks of Civility and Distinction from you. Conceal your Esteem and Love in your own Breast, and reserve your kind Looks and Language for Private hours; which are so many in the Four and Twenty, that they will afford time to employ a Passion as exalted as any that was ever
20 described in a French Romance.

Upon this Head, I should likewise advise you to differ in Practice from those Ladies who affect abundance of Uneasiness while their Husbands are abroad; start with every Knock at the Door, and ring the Bell incessantly for the Servants to let in their Master; will not eat a bit at Dinner or Supper if the Husband happens to stay out; and receive him at his return with such a Medley of chiding and kindness, and catechising him where he hath been, that a Shrew from Billingsgate would be a more easy and eligible Com-
30 panion.

Of the same leaven are those Wives, who when their Husbands are gone a Journey, must have a Letter every Post, upon pain of Fits and Hystericks; and a day must be fixed for their return home without the least allowance for Business, or Sickness, or Accidents, or Weather: Upon which,

I can only say that in my observation, those Ladies who are apt to make the greatest clutter upon such occasions, would liberally have paid a Messenger for bringing them news, that their Husbands had broken their Necks upon the Road.

You will perhaps be offended when I advise you to abate a little of that violent Passion for fine Cloaths, so predominant in your Sex. It is somewhat hard, that ours, for whose sake you wear them, are not admitted to be of your Council: I may venture to assure you that we will make an 10 abatement at any time of Four Pounds a yard in a Brocade, if the Ladies will but allow a suitable addition of care in the Cleanliness and Sweetness of their Persons: For, the satyrical part of mankind will needs believe, that it is not impossible, to be very fine and very filthy; and that the Capacities of a Lady are sometimes apt to fall short in cultivating Cleanliness and Finery together. I shall only add, upon so tender a subject, what a pleasant Gentleman said concerning a silly Woman of quality; that nothing could make her supportable but cutting off her Head; for his Ears were offended by her 20 Tongue, and his Nose by her Hair and Teeth.

But the Grand affair of your life will be to gain and preserve the Friendship and Esteem of your Husband. You are married to a Man of good education and learning, of an excellent understanding, and an exact taste. It is true, and it is happy for you, that these Qualities in him are adorned with great Modesty, a most amiable Sweetness of Temper, and an unusual disposition to Sobriety and Virtue: But neither Good-Nature nor Virtue will suffer him to esteem you against his Judgment; and although he be not capable 30 of using you ill, yet you will in time grow a thing indifferent, and perhaps, contemptible; unless you can supply the loss of Youth and Beauty with more durable Qualities. You have but a very few years to be young and handsome in the eyes of the World; and as few months to be so in the eyes of a Husband, who is not a Fool; for I hope you do not still dream of Charms and Raptures, which Marriage ever did, and ever will, put a sudden end to. Besides yours was a match of Prudence and common Good-liking, without any mixture of that ridiculous Passion which hath no Being, but in Play-Books and Romances.

You must, therefore, use all endeavours to attain to some degree of those Accomplishments, which your Husband most values in other People, and for which he is most valued
10 himself. You must improve your Mind, by closely pursuing such a Method of Study, as I shall direct or approve of. You must get a collection of History and Travels, which I will recommend to you; and spend some hours every day in reading them, and making extracts from them if your Memory be weak. You must invite Persons of knowledge and understanding to an acquaintance with you, by whose Conversation you may learn to correct your Taste and Judgment; and when you can bring yourself to comprehend and relish the good Sense of others, you will arrive, in time,
20 to think rightly yourself, and to become a Reasonable and Agreeable Companion. This must produce in your Husband a true Rational Love and Esteem for you, which old Age will not diminish. He will have a regard for your Judgment and Opinion, in matters of the greatest weight; you will be able to entertain each other without a Third Person to relieve you by finding Discourse. The endowments of your Mind will even make your Person more agreeable to him; and when you are alone, your Time will not lie heavy upon your hands, for want of some trifling Amusement.

30 I know very well that those who are commonly called Learned Women, have lost all manner of Credit by their impertinent Talkativeness and Conceit of themselves: but there is an easy remedy for this; if you once consider, that after all the pains you may be at, you never can arrive, in point of learning, to the perfection of a School-boy. But the

Reading I would advise you to, is only for improvement of your own good Sense, which will never fail of being Mended by Discretion. It is a wrong method, and ill choice of Books, that makes those Learned Ladies just so much worse for what they have read. And therefore it shall be my care to direct you better; a task for which I take my self to be not ill qualified; because I have spent more time, and have had more opportunities than many others, to observe and discover from what sources the various follies of Women are derived. 10

Pray observe how insignificant things are the common race of Ladies, when they have passed their Youth and Beauty; how contemptible they appear to the Men, and yet more contemptible to the younger part of their own Sex; and have no relief but in passing their afternoons in visits, where they are never acceptable; and their evenings at cards among each other; while the former part of the day is spent in spleen and envy, or in vain endeavours to repair by art and dress the ruins of Time: Whereas I have known Ladies at Sixty, to whom all the polite part of the Court and Town 20 paid their addresses; without any further view than that of enjoying the pleasure of their conversation.

I am ignorant of any one quality that is amiable in a Man, which is not equally so in a Woman: I do not except even Modesty and Gentleness of nature. Nor do I know one vice or folly, which is not equally detestable in both. There is indeed one infirmity which is generally allowed you, I mean that of Cowardice. Yet there should seem to be something very capricious, that when Women profess their admiration for a Colonel or a Captain on account of his Valour; they 30 should fancy it a very graceful becoming quality in themselves to be afraid of their own shadows; to scream in a Barge, when the weather is calmest, or in a Coach at the Ring; to run from a Cow at a hundred yards' distance; to fall into fits at the sight of a Spider, an Earwig, or a Frog.

At least, if Cowardice be a sign of Cruelty, (as it is generally granted) I can hardly think it an accomplishment so desirable as to be thought worth improving by Affectation.

And as the same Virtues equally become both Sexes, so there is no quality whereby Women endeavour to distinguish themselves from Men, for which they are not just so much the worse; except that only of Reservedness; which, however, as you generally manage it, is nothing else but Affectation or Hypocrisy. For, as you cannot too much discounte-
10 nance those of our Sex, who presume to take unbecoming liberty before you; so you ought to be wholly unconstrained in the company of Deserving Men, when you have had sufficient experience of their discretion.

I can give you no Advice upon the Article of Expence; only I think you ought to be well informed how much your Husband's Revenue amounts to, and be so good a Computer as to keep within it, in that part of the Management which falls to your share; and not to put yourself in the number of those Politick Ladies, who think they gain a great Point
20 when they have teazed their Husbands to buy them a new Equipage, a laced Head, or a fine Petticoat; without once considering what long Scores remain unpaid to the Butcher.

I desire you will keep this Letter in your Cabinet, and often examine impartially your whole Conduct by it: And so God bless you, and make you a fair Example to your Sex, and a perpetual Comfort to your Husband and your Parents.

I am, with great Truth and Affection,

Madam,

Your most faithful Friend

30 and humble Servant,

Jonath. Swift.

Deanry House, Febr. 11th, 1722–3

Drapier's Letter to Lord Molesworth, (1724)

To the Right Honourable the LORD VISCOUNT MOLESWORTH, at his House at *Brackdenstown* near *Swords*.

My Lord,
I Reflect too late on the Maxim of common Observers, that those who meddle in Matters out of their Calling, will have Reason to Repent; which is now verified in me: For by engaging in the Trade of a Writer, I have drawn upon my self the Displeasure of the Government, signified by a *Proclamation* promising a Reward of Three Hundred Pounds to the first *faithful* Subject who shall be able and inclined to 10 *inform* against me. To which I may add the laudable Zeal and Industry of my *Lord Chief Justice* in his Endeavours to discover so Dangerous a Person. Therefore whether I repent or no, I have certainly Cause to do so, and the common Observation still stands good.

It will sometimes happen, I know not how in the Course of Human Affairs, that a Man shall be made lyable to *Legal* Animadversions, where he has nothing to answer for, either to *God* or his *Country;* and condemned at *Westminster Hall* for what he will never be charged with at the *Day of* 20 *Judgment.*

After strictly examining my own Heart, and consulting some Divines of great Reputation, I cannot accuse my self of any *Malice* or *Wickedness against the Publick*; of any *Designs to Sow Sedition,* of *reflecting on the King and his Ministers,* or of endeavouring *to alienate the Affections of the People of this Kingdom from those of* England. All I can charge my self with, is a weak Attempt to serve a Nation in Danger of Destruction by a most wicked and malicious Projector, without waiting until I were called to its Assistance; 30 which Attempt, however it may perhaps give me the Title of *Pragmatical* and *Overweening,* will never lye a Burthen upon my Conscience. God knows whether I may not with all my caution have already run my self into Danger, by offering thus much in my own Vindication. For I have heard of a *Judge*, who, upon the Criminal's *Appeal* to the *Dreadful Day of Judgment*, told him he had incurred a *Premunire* for *appealing to a Foreign Jurisdiction:* And of another in *Wales*, who severely checked the Prisoner for offering the same Plea, taxing him with reflecting on the Court by such a Comparison, because *Comparisons were odious*.

10 But in Order to make some Excuse for being more speculative than others of my Condition, I desire your Lordship's Pardon, while I am doing a very foolish thing, which is, to give you some little Account of my self.

I was bred at a Free-School where I acquired some little Knowledge in the *Latin Tongue*, I served my Apprenticeship in *London*, and there set up for my self with good Success, 'till by the *Death of some Friends, and the Misfortunes of Others*, I returned into this Kingdom, and began to employ my Thoughts in cultivating the *Woollen Manufacture* 20 through all it's Branches. Wherein I met with great Discouragement and Powerful Opposers, whose Objections appeared to me very strange and singular. They argued that the People of *England* would be offended if our Manufactures were brought to *equal* theirs; and even some of the *Weaving* Trade were my Enemies, which I could not but look upon as *absurd* and *unnatural*. I remember your Lordship at that time did me the Honour to come into my Shop, where I shewed you a Piece of *Black and White Stuff* just sent from the *Dyer*, which you were pleased to approve of, and be my 30 Customer for it.

However I was so mortified, that I resolved for the future to sit quietly in my Shop, and Deal in *Common Goods* like the rest of my Brethren. Till it happened some Months ago considering with my self that the *lower and poorer Sort of People* wanted a *plain strong course Stuff to defend them against cold Easterly Winds, which then blew very fierce and blasting for a long time together,* I contrived one on purpose, which sold very well all over the Kingdom, and preserved many Thousands from *Agues*. I then made a *Second* and a *Third* kind of *Stuffs* for the *Gentry* with the same Success, insomuch that an *Ague* hath hardly been heard of for some time.

This incited me so far, that I ventured upon a *Fourth* Piece made of the best *Irish* Wooll I could get, and I thought it Grave and Rich enough to be worn by the best *Lord* or *Judge* of the Land. But of late some *Great Folks* complain as I hear, that when they had it on, they felt a *Shuddering in their Limbs,* and have thrown it off in a Rage, cursing to Hell the poor *Drapier* who invented it, so that I am determined never to *work for Persons of Quality* again, except for your *Lordship* and a *very few more.*

I assure your Lordship upon the Word of an Honest Citizen, that I am not Richer by the Value of one of Mr. *Wood*'s Half-pence with the Sale of all the several *Stuffs* I have contrived; for I give the whole Profit to the *Dyers* and *Pressers*. And therefore I hope you will please to believe, that no other Motive beside the Love of my Country could engage me to busie my Head and Hands to the Loss of my Time and the Gain of nothing but *Vexation* and *Ill Will.*

I have now in Hand one *Piece of Stuff* to be woven on purpose for your Lordship, although I might be ashamed to offer it you, after I have confessed that it will be made only from the *Shreds and Remnants of the Wooll employed in the Former*. However I shall *work* it up as well as I can, and at worst, you need only give it among your Tenants.

I am very sensible how ill your Lordship is like to be entertained with the Pedantry of a *Drapier* in the Terms of his own Trade. How will the Matter be mended, when you find me entring again, though very sparingly, into an Affair of State; For such is now grown the Controversie with Mr.

Wood, if *some great Lawyers* are to be Credited. And as it often happens at Play, that Men begin with *Farthings,* and go on to *Gold,* till some of them lose their Estates and dye in Jayl; so it may possibly fall out in my Case, that by *playing* too long with Mr. *Wood's* Half-pence, I may be drawn in to pay a *Fine,* double to the Reward for *Betraying* me, be sent to Prison, and *not to be delivered thence 'till I shall have payed the uttermost Farthing.*

There are my Lord, three sorts of Persons with whom I am
10 resolved never to dispute; A *High-way-man* with a Pistol at my Breast, a *Troop of Dragoons* who come to plunder my House, and a *Man of the Law* who can make a *Merit* of accusing me. In each of these Cases, *which are almost the same,* the best Method is to *keep out of the Way,* and the next Best is to *deliver your Money, surrender your House,* and *confess nothing.*

GULLIVER'S TRAVELS

A Letter from Captain Gulliver to his Cousin Sympson

I HOPE you will be ready to own publickly, whenever you shall be called to it, that by your great and frequent Urgency you prevailed on me to publish a very loose and uncorrect Account of my Travels; with Direction to hire some young Gentlemen of either University to put them in Order, and correct the Style, as my Cousin *Dampier* did by my Advice, in his Book called, *A Voyage round the World*. But I do not remember I gave you Power to consent, that any thing should be omitted, and much less that any thing should be inserted: Therefore, as to the latter, I do here renounce every thing of that Kind; particularly a Paragraph about her Majesty the late Queen *Anne*, of most pious and glorious Memory; although I did reverence and esteem her more than any of human Species. But you, or your Interpolator, ought to have considered, that as it was not my Inclination, so was it not decent to praise any Animal of our Composition before my Master *Houyhnhnm*: And besides, the Fact was altogether false; for to my Knowledge, being in *England* during some Part of her Majesty's Reign, she did govern by a chief Minister; nay, even by two successively; the first whereof was the Lord of *Godolphin*, and the second the Lord of *Oxford*; so that you have made me *say the thing that was not*. Likewise, in the Account of the Academy of Projectors, and several Passages of my Discourse to my Master *Houyhnhnm*, you have either omitted some material Circumstances, or minced or changed them in such a Manner, that I do hardly know mine own Work. When I formerly hinted to you something of this in a Letter, you were pleased to answer, that you were afraid of giving Offence; that People in Power were very watchful over the Press; and apt not only to interpret, but to punish every thing which looked like an *Inuendo* (as I think you called it.) But pray, how could that which I spoke so many Years ago, and at above five Thousand Leagues distance, in another Reign, be applyed to any of the *Yahoos*, who now are said to govern the Herd; especially, at a time when I little thought on or feared the Unhappiness of living under them. Have not I the most Reason to complain, when I see these very *Yahoos* carried by *Houyhnhnms* in a Vehicle, as if these were Brutes, and those the rational Creatures? And, indeed, to avoid so monstrous and detestable a Sight, was one principal Motive of my Retirement hither.

Thus much I thought proper to tell you in Relation to your self, and to the Trust I reposed in you.

I do in the next Place complain of my own great Want of Judgment, in being prevailed upon by the Intreaties and false Reasonings of you and some others, very much against mine own Opinion, to suffer my Travels to be published. Pray bring to your Mind how often I desired you to consider, when you insisted on the Motive of *publick Good*; that the *Yahoos* were a Species of Animals utterly incapable of Amendment by Precepts or Examples: And so it hath proved; for instead of seeing a full Stop put to all Abuses and Corruptions, at least in this little Island, as I had Reason to expect: Behold, after above six Months Warning, I cannot learn that my Book hath produced one single Effect according to mine Intentions: I desired you would let me know by a Letter, when Party and Faction were extinguished; Judges learned and upright; Pleaders honest and modest, with some Tincture of common Sense; and *Smithfield* blazing with Pyramids of Law-Books; the young Nobility's Education entirely changed; the Physicians banished; the Female *Yahoos* abounding in Virtue, Honour, Truth and good Sense: Courts and Levees of great Ministers thoroughly weeded and swept; Wit, Merit and Learning rewarded; all Disgracers of the Press in Prose and Verse, condemned to eat nothing but their own Cotten, and quench their Thirst with their own Ink. These, and a Thousand other Reformations, I firmly counted upon by your Encouragement; as indeed they were plainly deducible from the Precepts delivered in my Book. And, it must be owned, that seven Months were a sufficient Time to correct every Vice and Folly to which *Yahoos* are subject; if their Natures had been capable of the least Disposition to Virtue or Wisdom: Yet so far have you been from answering mine Expectation in any of your Letters; that on the contrary, you are loading our Carrier every Week with Libels, and Keys, and Reflections, and Memoirs, and Second Parts; wherein I see myself accused of reflecting upon great States-Folk; of degrading human Nature, (for so they have still the Confidence to stile it) and of abusing the Female Sex. I find likewise, that the Writers of those Bundles are not agreed among themselves; for some of them will not allow me to be Author of mine own Travels; and others make me Author of Books to which I am wholly a Stranger.

I find likewise, that your Printer hath been so careless as to confound the Times, and mistake the Dates of my several Voyages and Returns; neither assigning the true Year, or the true Month, or Day of the Month: And I hear the original Manuscript is all destroyed, since the Publication of my Book. Neither have I any Copy left; however, I have sent you some Corrections, which you may insert, if ever there should be a second Edition: And yet I cannot stand to them, but shall leave that Matter to my judicious and candid Readers, to adjust it as they please.

I hear some of our Sea-*Yahoos* find Fault with my Sea-Language, as not proper in many Parts, nor now in Use. I cannot help it. In my first Voyages, while I was young, I was instructed by the oldest Mariners, and learned to speak as they did. But I have since found that the Sea-*Yahoos* are apt, like the Land ones, to become new fangled in their Words; which the latter change every Year; insomuch, as I remember upon each Return to mine own Country, their old Dialect was so altered, that I could hardly understand the new. And I observe, when any *Yahoo* comes from *London* out of Curiosity to visit me at mine own House, we neither of us are able to deliver our Conceptions in a Manner intelligible to the other.

If the Censure of *Yahoos* could any Way affect me, I
10 should have great Reason to complain, that some of them are so bold as to think my Book of Travels a meer Fiction out of mine own Brain; and have gone so far as to drop Hints, that the *Houyhnhnms* and *Yahoos* have no more Existence than the Inhabitants of *Utopia.*

Indeed I must confess, that as to the People of *Lilliput, Brobdingrag,* (for so the Word should have been spelt, and not erroneously *Brobdingnag*) and *Laputa*; I have never yet heard of any *Yahoo* so presumptuous as to dispute their Being, or the Facts I have related concerning them; because
20 the Truth immediately strikes every Reader with Conviction. And, is there less Probability in my Account of the *Houyhnhnms* or *Yahoos,* when it is manifest as to the latter, there are so many Thousands in this City, who only differ from their Brother Brutes in *Houyhnhnmland,* because they use a Sort of *Jabber,* and do not go naked. I wrote for their Amendment, and not their Approbation. The united Praise of the whole Race would be of less Consequence to me, than the neighing of those two degenerate *Houyhnhnms* I keep in my Stable; because, from these, degenerate as they are, I
30 still improve in some Virtues, without any Mixture of Vice.

Do these miserable Animals presume to think that I am so far degenerated as to defend my Veracity; *Yahoo* as I am, it is well known through all *Houyhnhnmland,* that by the Instructions and Example of my illustrious Master, I was able in the Compass of two Years (although I confess with the utmost Difficulty) to remove that infernal Habit of Lying, Shuffling, Deceiving, and Equivocating, so deeply rooted in the very Souls of all my Species; especially the *Europeans*.

I have other Complaints to make upon this vexatious Occasion; but I forbear troubling myself or you any further. I must freely confess, that since my last Return, some corruptions of my *Yahoo* Nature have revived in me by Conversing with a few of your Species, and particularly those of mine own Family, by an unavoidable Necessity; 10 else I should never have attempted so absurd a Project as that of reforming the *Yahoo* Race in this Kingdom; but, I have now done with all such visionary Schemes for ever.

April 2, 1727.

(But first printed and probably written for Faulkner's ed. 1735.)

The Publisher to the Reader

THE Author of these Travels, Mr. *Lemuel Gulliver*, is my antient and intimate Friend; there is likewise some Relation between us by the Mother's Side. About three Years ago Mr. *Gulliver* growing weary of the Concourse of curious People coming to him at his House in *Redriff*, made a small Purchase of Land, with a convenient House, near *Newark*, in *Nottinghamshire*, his native Country; where he now lives 20 retired, yet in good Esteem among his Neighbours.

Although Mr. *Gulliver* was born in *Nottinghamshire*, where his Father dwelt, yet I have heard him say, his Family came from *Oxfordshire*; to confirm which, I have observed in the Church-Yard at *Banbury*, in that County, several Tombs and Monuments of the *Gullivers*.

Before he quitted *Redriff*, he left the Custody of the following Papers in my Hands, with the Liberty to dispose of them as I should think fit. I have carefully perused them 30 three Times: The Style is very plain and simple; and the only Fault I find is, that the Author, after the Manner of Travellers, is a little too circumstantial. There is an Air of Truth apparent through the whole; and indeed the Author was so distinguished for his Veracity, that it became a Sort of Proverb among his Neighbours at *Redriff*, when any one affirmed a Thing, to say, it was as true as if Mr. *Gulliver* had spoke it.

By the Advice of several worthy Persons, to whom, with 10 the Author's Permission, I communicated these Papers, I now venture to send them into the World; hoping they may be, at least for some time, a better Entertainment to our young Noblemen, than the common Scribbles of Politicks and Party.

This Volume would have been at least twice as large, if I had not made bold to strike out innumerable Passages relating to the Winds and Tides, as well as to the Variations and Bearings in the several Voyages; together with the minute Descriptions of the Management of the Ship in Storms, in the 20 Style of Sailors: Likewise the Account of the Longitudes and Latitudes; wherein I have Reason to apprehend that Mr. *Gulliver* may be a little dissatisfied: But I was resolved to fit the Work as much as possible to the general Capacity of Readers. However, if my own Ignorance in Sea-Affairs shall have led me to commit some Mistakes, I alone am answerable for them: And if any Traveller hath a Curiosity to see the whole Work at large, as it came from the Hand of the Author, I will be ready to gratify him.

As for any further Particulars relating to the Author, the 30 Reader will receive Satisfaction from the first Pages of the Book.

Richard Sympson.

A Voyage to Lilliput, Chapter I

The Author giveth some Account of himself and Family; his first Inducements to travel. He is shipwrecked, and swims for his Life; gets safe on shoar in the Country of Lilliput, *is made a Prisoner, and carried up the Country.*

MY Father had a small Estate in *Nottinghamshire*; I was the Third of five Sons. He sent me to *Emanuel-College* in *Cambridge*, at Fourteen Years old, where I resided three Years, and applied my self close to my Studies: But the Charge of maintaining me (although I had a very scanty Allowance) being too great for a narrow Fortune; I was bound Apprentice to Mr. *James Bates*, an eminent Surgeon in *London*, with whom I continued four Years; and my Father now and then sending me small Sums of Money, I laid them out in learning Navigation, and other Parts of the Mathematicks, useful to those who intend to travel, as I always believed it would be some time or other my Fortune to do. When I left Mr. *Bates*, I went down to my Father; where, by the Assistance of him and my Uncle *John*, and some other Relations, I got Forty Pounds, and a Promise of Thirty Pounds a Year to maintain me at *Leyden*: There I studied Physick two Years and seven Months, knowing it would be useful in long Voyages.

Soon after my Return from *Leyden*, I was recommended by my good Master Mr. *Bates*, to be Surgeon to the *Swallow*, Captain *Abraham Pannell* Commander; with whom I continued three Years and a half, making a Voyage or two into the *Levant*, and some other Parts. When I came back, I resolved to settle in *London*, to which Mr. *Bates*, my Master, encouraged me; and by him I was recommended to several Patients. I took Part of a small House in the *Old Jury*; and being advised to alter my Condition, I married Mrs. *Mary Burton*, second Daughter to Mr. *Edmond Burton*, Hosier, in *Newgate-street*, with whom I received four Hundred Pounds for a Portion.

But, my good Master *Bates* dying in two Years after, and I having few Friends, my Business began to fail; for my Conscience would not suffer me to imitate the bad Practice of too many among my Brethren. Having therefore consulted with my Wife, and some of my Acquaintance, I determined to go again to Sea. I was Surgeon successively in two Ships, and made several Voyages, for six Years, to the *East* and *West-Indies*; by which I got some Addition to my Fortune. My Hours of Leisure I spent in reading the best
10 Authors, ancient and modern; being always provided with a good Number of Books; and when I was ashore, in observing the Manners and Dispositions of the People, as well as learning their Language; wherein I had a great Facility by the Strength of my Memory.

The last of these Voyages not proving very fortunate, I grew weary of the Sea, and intended to stay at home with my Wife and Family. I removed from the *Old Jury* to *Fetter-Lane*, and from thence to *Wapping*, hoping to get Business among the Sailors; but it would not turn to account. After
20 three Years Expectation that things would mend, I accepted an advantageous Offer from Captain *William Prichard*, Master of the *Antelope*, who was making a Voyage to the *South-Sea*. We set sail from *Bristol*, *May* 4th, 1699, and our Voyage at first was very prosperous.

It would not be proper for some Reasons, to trouble the Reader with the Particulars of our Adventures in those Seas: Let it suffice to inform him, that in our Passage from thence to the *East-Indies*, we were driven by a violent Storm to the North-west of *Van Diemen*'s Land. By an Observation,
30 we found ourselves in the Latitude of 30 Degrees 2 Minutes South. Twelve of our Crew were dead by immoderate Labour, and ill Food; the rest were in a very weak Condition. On the fifth of *November*, which was the beginning of Summer in those Parts, the Weather being very hazy, the Seamen spyed a Rock, within half a Cable's length of the

Ship; but the Wind was so strong, that we were driven directly upon it, and immediately split. Six of the Crew, of whom I was one, having let down the Boat into the Sea, made a Shift to get clear of the Ship, and the Rock. We rowed by my Computation, about three Leagues, till we were able to work no longer, being already spent with Labour while we were in the Ship. We therefore trusted ourselves to the Mercy of the Waves; and in about half an Hour the Boat was overset by a sudden Flurry from the North. What became of my Companions in the Boat, as well as of 10 those who escaped on the Rock, or were left in the Vessel, I cannot tell; but conclude they were all lost. For my own Part, I swam as Fortune directed me, and was pushed forward by Wind and Tide. I often let my Legs drop, and could feel no Bottom: But when I was almost gone, and able to struggle no longer, I found myself within my Depth; and by this Time the Storm was much abated. The Declivity was so small, that I walked near a Mile before I got to the Shore, which I conjectured was about Eight o'Clock in the Evening. I then advanced forward near half a Mile, but could not 20 discover any Sign of Houses or Inhabitants; at least I was in so weak a Condition, that I did not observe them. I was extremely tired, and with that, and the Heat of the Weather, and about half a Pint of Brandy that I drank as I left the Ship, I found my self much inclined to sleep. I lay down on the Grass, which was very short and soft; where I slept sounder than ever I remember to have done in my Life, and as I reckoned, above Nine Hours; for when I awaked, it was just Day-light. I attempted to rise, but was not able to stir: For as I happened to lie on my Back, I found my Arms and 30 Legs were strongly fastened on each Side to the Ground; and my Hair, which was long and thick, tied down in the same Manner. I likewise felt several slender Ligatures across my Body, from my Armpits to my Thighs. I could only look upwards; the Sun began to grow hot, and the Light offended mine Eyes. I heard a confused Noise about me, but in the Posture I lay, could see nothing except the Sky. In a little time I felt something alive moving on my left Leg, which advancing gently forward over my Breast, came almost up to my Chin; when bending mine Eyes downwards as much as I could, I perceived it to be a human Creature not six Inches high, with a Bow and Arrow in his Hands, and a Quiver at his Back. In the mean time, I felt at least Forty more of the same Kind (as I conjectured) following the first. I was in the utmost Astonishment, and roared so loud, that they all ran back in a Fright; and some of them, as I was afterwards told, were hurt with the Falls they got by leaping from my Sides upon the Ground. However, they soon returned; and one of them, who ventured so far as to get a full Sight of my Face, lifting up his Hands and Eyes by way of Admiration, cryed out in a shrill, but distinct Voice, *Hekinah Degul*: The others repeated the same Words several times, but I then knew not what they meant. I lay all this while, as the Reader may believe, in great Uneasiness: At length, struggling to get loose, I had the Fortune to break the Strings, and wrench out the Pegs that fastened my left Arm to the Ground; for, by lifting it up to my Face, I discovered the Methods they had taken to bind me; and, at the same time, with a violent Pull, which gave me excessive Pain, I a little loosened the Strings that tied down my Hair on the left Side; so that I was just able to turn my Head about two Inches. But the Creatures ran off a second time, before I could seize them; whereupon there was a great Shout in a very shrill Accent; and after it ceased, I heard one of them cry aloud, *Tolgo Phonac*; when in an Instant I felt above an Hundred Arrows discharged on my left Hand, which pricked me like so many Needles; and besides, they shot another Flight into the Air, as we do Bombs in *Europe*; whereof many, I suppose, fell on my Body, (though I felt them not) and some on my Face, which I immediately covered with my left Hand. When this Shower of Arrows was over, I fell a groaning with Grief and Pain; and then striving again to get loose, they discharged another Volly larger than the first; and some of them attempted with Spears to stick me in the Sides; but, by good Luck, I had on me a Buff Jerkin, which they could not pierce. I thought it the most prudent Method to lie still; and my Design was to continue so till Night, when my left Hand being already loose, I could easily free myself: And as for the Inhabitants, I had Reason to believe I might be a Match for the greatest Armies they 10 could bring against me, if they were all of the same Size with him that I saw. But Fortune disposed otherwise of me. When the People observed I was quiet, they discharged no more Arrows: But by the Noise increasing, I knew their Numbers were greater; and about four Yards from me, over-against my right Ear, I heard a Knocking for above an Hour, like People at work; when turning my Head that Way, as well as the Pegs and Strings would permit me, I saw a Stage erected about a Foot and a half from the Ground, capable of holding four of the Inhabitants, with two or three 20 Ladders to mount it: From whence one of them, who seemed to be a Person of Quality, made me a long Speech, whereof I understood not one Syllable. But I should have mentioned, that before the principal Person began his Oration, he cryed out three times *Langro Dehul san*: (these Words and the former were afterwards repeated and explained to me.) Whereupon immediately about fifty of the Inhabitants came, and cut the Strings that fastened the left side of my Head, which gave me the Liberty of turning it to the right, and of observing the Person and Gesture of 30 him who was to speak. He appeared to be of a middle Age, and taller than any of the other three who attended him; whereof one was a Page, who held up his Train, and seemed to be somewhat longer than my middle Finger; the other two stood one on each side to support him. He acted every part of an Orator; and I could observe many Periods of Threatnings, and others of Promises, Pity, and Kindness. I answered in a few Words, but in the most submissive Manner, lifting up my left Hand and both mine Eyes to the Sun, as calling him for a Witness; and being almost famished with Hunger, having not eaten a Morsel for some Hours before I left the Ship, I found the Demands of Nature so strong upon me, that I could not forbear shewing my Impatience (perhaps against the strict Rules of Decency) by putting my Finger frequently on my Mouth, to signify that I wanted Food. The *Hurgo* (for so they call a great Lord, as I afterwards learnt) understood me very well: He descended from the Stage, and commanded that several Ladders should be applied to my Sides, on which above an hundred of the Inhabitants mounted, and walked towards my Mouth, laden with Baskets full of Meat, which had been provided, and sent thither by the King's Orders upon the first Intelligence he received of me. I observed there was the Flesh of several Animals, but could not distinguish them by the Taste. There were Shoulders, Legs, and Loins shaped like those of Mutton, and very well dressed, but smaller than the Wings of a Lark. I eat them by two or three at a Mouthful; and took three Loaves at a time, about the bigness of Musket Bullets. They supplyed me as fast as they could, shewing a thousand Marks of Wonder and Astonishment at my Bulk and Appetite. I then made another Sign that I wanted Drink. They found by my eating that a small Quantity would not suffice me; and being a most ingenious People, they slung up with great Dexterity one of their largest Hogsheads; then rolled it towards my Hand, and beat out the Top; I drank it off at a Draught, which I might well do, for it hardly held half a Pint, and tasted like a small Wine of *Burgundy*, but much more delicious. They brought me a second Hogshead, which I drank in the same Manner, and made Signs for more, but they had none to give me. When

I had performed these Wonders, they shouted for Joy, and danced upon my Breast, repeating several times as they did at first, *Hekinah Degul*. They made me a Sign that I should throw down the two Hogsheads, but first warned the People below to stand out of the Way, crying aloud, *Borach Mivola*; and when they saw the Vessels in the Air, there was an universal Shout of *Hekinah Degul*. I confess I was often tempted, while they were passing backwards and forwards on my Body, to seize Forty or Fifty of the first that came in my Reach, and dash them against the Ground. But the 10 Remembrance of what I had felt, which probably might not be the worst they could do; and the Promise of Honour I made them, for so I interpreted my submissive Behaviour, soon drove out those Imaginations. Besides, I now considered my self as bound by the Laws of Hospitality to a People who had treated me with so much Expence and Magnificence. However, in my Thoughts I could not sufficiently wonder at the Intrepidity of these diminutive Mortals, who durst venture to mount and walk on my Body, while one of my Hands was at Liberty, without trembling at 20 the very Sight of so prodigious a Creature as I must appear to them. After some time, when they observed that I made no more Demands for Meat, there appeared before me a Person of high Rank from his Imperial Majesty. His Excellency having mounted on the Small of my Right Leg, advanced forwards up to my Face, with about a Dozen of his Retinue; And producing his Credentials under the Signet Royal, which he applied close to mine Eyes, spoke about ten Minutes, without any Signs of Anger, but with a kind of determinate Resolution; often pointing forwards, which, as 30 I afterwards found was towards the Capital City, about half a Mile distant, whither it was agreed by his Majesty in Council that I must be conveyed. I answered in few Words, but to no Purpose, and made a Sign with my Hand that was loose, putting it to the other, (but over his Excellency's

Head, for Fear of hurting him or his Train) and then to my own Head and Body, to signify that I desired my Liberty. It appeared that he understood me well enough; for he shook his Head by way of Disapprobation, and held his Hand in a Posture to shew that I must be carried as a Prisoner. However, he made other Signs to let me understand that I should have Meat and Drink enough, and very good Treatment. Whereupon I once more thought of attempting to break my Bonds; but again, when I felt the Smart of their Arrows upon my Face and Hands, which were all in Blisters, and many of the Darts still sticking in them; and observing likewise that the Number of my Enemies encreased; I gave Tokens to let them know that they might do with me what they pleased. Upon this, the *Hurgo* and his Train withdrew, with much Civility and chearful Countenances. Soon after I heard a general Shout, with frequent Repetitions of the Words, *Peplom Selan,* and I felt great Numbers of the People on my Left Side relaxing the Cords to such a Degree, that I was able to turn upon my Right, and to ease my self with making Water; which I very plentifully did, to the great Astonishment of the People, who conjecturing by my Motions what I was going to do, immediately opened to the right and left on that Side, to avoid the Torrent which fell with such Noise and Violence from me. But before this, they had dawbed my Face and both my Hands with a sort of Ointment very pleasant to the Smell, which in a few Minutes removed all the Smart of their Arrows. These Circumstances, added to the Refreshment I had received by their Victuals and Drink, which were very nourishing, disposed me to sleep. I slept about eight Hours as I was afterwards assured; and it was no Wonder; for the Physicians, by the Emperor's Order, had mingled a sleeping Potion in the Hogsheads of Wine.

It seems that upon the first Moment I was discovered sleeping on the Ground after my Landing, the Emperor had early Notice of it by an Express; and determined in Council that I should be tyed in the Manner I have related (which was done in the Night while I slept) that Plenty of Meat and Drink should be sent me, and a Machine prepared to carry me to the Capital City.

This Resolution perhaps may appear very bold and dangerous, and I am confident would not be imitated by any Prince in *Europe* on the like Occasion; however, in my Opinion it was extremely Prudent as well as Generous. For supposing these People had endeavoured to kill me with their 10 Spears and Arrows while I was asleep; I should certainly have awaked with the first Sense of Smart, which might so far have rouzed my Rage and Strength, as to enable me to break the Strings wherewith I was tyed; after which, as they were not able to make Resistance, so they could expect no Mercy.

These People are most excellent Mathematicians, and arrived to a great Perfection in Mechanicks by the Countenance and Encouragement of the Emperor, who is a renowned Patron of Learning. This Prince hath several Machines fixed 20 on Wheels, for the Carriage of Trees and other great Weights. He often buildeth his largest Men of War, whereof some are Nine Foot long, in the Woods where the Timber grows, and has them carried on these Engines three or four Hundred Yards to the Sea. Five Hundred Carpenters and Engineers were immediately set at work to prepare the greatest Engine they had. It was a Frame of Wood raised three Inches from the Ground, about seven Foot long and four wide, moving upon twenty two Wheels. The Shout I heard, was upon the Arrival of this Engine, which, it seems, set out in four Hours 30 after my Landing. It was brought parallel to me as I lay. But the principal Difficulty was to raise and place me in this Vehicle. Eighty Poles, each of one Foot high, were erected for this Purpose, and very strong Cords of the bigness of Packthread were fastened by Hooks to many Bandages, which the Workmen had girt round my Neck, my Hands, my Body, and my Legs. Nine Hundred of the strongest Men were employed to draw up these Cords by many Pullies fastned on the Poles; and thus in less than three Hours, I was raised and slung into the Engine, and there tyed fast. All this I was told; for while the whole Operation was performing, I lay in a profound Sleep, by the Force of that soporiferous Medicine infused into my Liquor. Fifteen hundred of the Emperor's largest Horses, each about four Inches and a half high, were employed to draw me towards the Metropolis, which, as I said, was half a Mile distant.

About four Hours after we began our Journey, I awaked by a very ridiculous Accident; for the Carriage being stopt a while to adjust something that was out of Order, two or three of the young Natives had the Curiosity to see how I looked when I was asleep; they climbed up into the Engine, and advancing very softly to my Face, one of them, an Officer in the Guards, put the sharp End of his Half-Pike a good way up into my left Nostril, which tickled my Nose like a Straw, and made me sneeze violently: Whereupon they stole off unperceived; and it was three Weeks before I knew the Cause of my awaking so suddenly. We made a long March the remaining Part of the Day, and rested at Night with Five Hundred Guards on each Side of me, half with Torches, and half with Bows and Arrows, ready to shoot me if I should offer to stir. The next Morning at Sunrise we continued our March, and arrived within two Hundred Yards of the City-Gates about Noon. The Emperor, and all his Court, came out to meet us; but his great Officers would by no means suffer his Majesty to endanger his Person by mounting on my Body.

At the Place where the Carriage stopt, there stood an ancient Temple, esteemed to be the largest in the whole Kingdom; which having been polluted some Years before by an unnatural Murder, was, according to the Zeal of those

People, looked upon as Prophane, and therefore had been applied to common Use, and all the Ornaments and Furniture carried away. In this Edifice it was determined I should lodge. The great Gate fronting to the North was about four Foot high, and almost two Foot wide, through which I could easily creep. On each Side of the Gate was a small Window not above six Inches from the Ground: Into that on the Left Side, the King's Smiths conveyed fourscore and eleven Chains, like those that hang to a Lady's Watch in *Europe*, and almost as large, which were locked to my Left 10 Leg with six and thirty Padlocks. Over against this Temple, on the other Side of the great Highway, at twenty Foot Distance, there was a Turret at least five Foot high. Here the Emperor ascended with many principal Lords of his Court, to have an Opportunity of viewing me, as I was told, for I could not see them. It was reckoned that above an hundred thousand Inhabitants came out of the Town upon the same Errand; and in spight of my Guards, I believe there could not be fewer than ten thousand, at several Times, who mounted upon my Body by the Help of Ladders. But a Pro- 20 clamation was soon issued to forbid it, upon Pain of Death. When the Workmen found it was impossible for me to break loose, they cut all the Strings that bound me; whereupon I rose up with as melancholly a Disposition as ever I had in my Life. But the Noise and Astonishment of the People at seeing me rise and walk, are not to be expressed. The Chains that held my left Leg were about two Yards long, and gave me not only the Liberty of walking backwards and forwards in a Semicircle; but being fixed within four Inches of the Gate, allowed me to creep in, and lie at my full Length in the 30 Temple.

A Voyage to Brobdingnag, Chapter VI

Several Contrivances of the Author to please the King and Queen. He shews his Skill in Musick. The King enquires into the State of Europe, *which the Author relates to him. The King's Observations thereon.*

I USED to attend the King's Levee once or twice a Week, and had often seen him under the Barber's Hand, which indeed was at first very terrible to behold. For, the Razor was almost twice as long as an ordinary Scythe. His Majesty, according to the Custom of the Country, was only shaved twice a Week. I once prevailed on the Barber to give me
10 some of the Suds or Lather, out of which I picked Forty or Fifty of the strongest Stumps of Hair. I then took a Piece of fine Wood, and cut it like the Back of a Comb, making several Holes in it at equal Distance, with as small a Needle as I could get from *Glumdalclitch*. I fixed in the Stumps so artificially, scraping and sloping them with my Knife towards the Points, that I made a very tolerable Comb; which was a seasonable Supply, my own being so much broken in the Teeth, that it was almost useless: Neither did I know any Artist in that Country so nice and exact, as would under-
20 take to make me another.

And this puts me in mind of an Amusement wherein I spent many of my leisure Hours. I desired the Queen's Woman to save for me the Combings of her Majesty's Hair, whereof in time I got a good Quantity; and consulting with my Friend the Cabinet-maker, who had received general Orders to do little Jobbs for me; I directed him to make two Chair-frames, no larger than those I had in my Box, and then to bore little Holes with a fine Awl round those Parts where I designed the Backs and Seats; through these Holes
30 I wove the strongest Hairs I could pick out, just after the Manner of Cane-chairs in *England*. When they were finished, I made a Present of them to her Majesty, who kept them in her Cabinet, and used to shew them for Curiosities; as indeed

they were the Wonder of every one who beheld them. The Queen would have had me sit upon one of these Chairs, but I absolutely refused to obey her; protesting I would rather dye a Thousand Deaths than place a dishonourable Part of my Body on those precious Hairs that once adorned her Majesty's Head. Of these Hairs (as I had always a Mechanical Genius) I likewise made a neat little Purse about five Foot long, with her Majesty's Name decyphered in Gold Letters; which I gave to *Glumdalclitch*, by the Queen's Consent. To say the Truth, it was more for Shew than Use, being not of 10 Strength to bear the Weight of the larger Coins; and therefore she kept nothing in it, but some little Toys that Girls are fond of.

The King, who delighted in Musick, had frequent Consorts at Court, to which I was sometimes carried, and set in my Box on a Table to hear them: But, the Noise was so great, that I could hardly distinguish the Tunes. I am confident, that all the Drums and Trumpets of a Royal Army, beating and sounding together just at your Ears, could not equal it. My Practice was to have my Box removed from the Places 20 where the Performers sat, as far as I could; then to shut the Doors and Windows of it, and draw the Window-Curtains; after which I found their Musick not disagreeable.

I had learned in my Youth to play a little upon the Spinet; *Glumdalclitch* kept one in her Chamber, and a Master attended twice a Week to teach her: I call it a Spinet, because it somewhat resembled that Instrument, and was play'd upon in the same Manner. A Fancy came into my Head, that I would entertain the King and Queen with an *English* Tune upon this Instrument. But this appeared extremely difficult: 30 For, the Spinet was near sixty Foot long, each Key being almost a Foot wide; so that, with my Arms extended, I could not reach to above five Keys; and to press them down required a good smart stroak with my Fist, which would be too great a Labour, and to no purpose. The Method I

contrived was this. I prepared two round Sticks about the Bigness of common Cudgels; they were thicker at one End than the other; and I covered the thicker End with a Piece of a Mouse's Skin, that by rapping on them, I might neither Damage the Tops of the Keys, nor interrupt the Sound. Before the Spinet, a Bench was placed about four Foot below the Keys, and I was put upon the Bench. I ran sideling upon it that way and this, as fast as I could, banging the proper Keys with my two Sticks; and made a shift to
10 play a Jigg to the great Satisfaction of both their Majesties: But, it was the most violent Exercise I ever underwent, and yet I could not strike above sixteen Keys, nor, consequently, play the Bass and Treble together, as other Artists do; which was a great Disadvantage to my Performance.

The King, who as I before observed, was a Prince of excellent Understanding, would frequently order that I should be brought in my Box, and set upon the Table in his Closet. He would then command me to bring one of my Chairs out of the Box, and sit down within three Yards Dis-
20 tance upon the Top of the Cabinet; which brought me almost to a Level with his Face. In this Manner I had several Conversations with him. I one Day took the Freedom to tell his Majesty, that the Contempt he discovered towards *Europe*, and the rest of the World, did not seem answerable to those excellent Qualities of Mind, that he was Master of. That, Reason did not extend itself with the Bulk of the Body: On the contrary, we observed in our Country, that the tallest Persons were usually least provided with it. That among other Animals, Bees and Ants had the Reputation of more
30 Industry, Art, and Sagacity than many of the larger Kinds. And that, as inconsiderable as he took me to be, I hoped I might live to do his Majesty some signal Service. The King heard me with Attention; and began to conceive a much better Opinion of me than he had ever before. He desired I would give him as exact an Account of the Government of

England as I possibly could; because, as fond as Princes commonly are of their own Customs (for so he conjectured of other Monarchs by my former Discourses) he should be glad to hear of any thing that might deserve Imitation.

Imagine with thy self, courteous Reader, how often I then wished for the Tongue of *Demosthenes* or *Cicero*, that might have enabled me to celebrate the Praise of my own dear native Country in a Style equal to its Merits and Felicity.

I began my Discourse by informing his Majesty, that our 10
Dominions consisted of two Islands, which composed three mighty Kingdoms under one Sovereign, besides our Plantations in *America*. I dwelt long upon the Fertility of our Soil, and the Temperature of our Climate. I then spoke at large upon the Constitution of an *English* Parliament, partly made up of an illustrious Body called the House of Peers, Persons of the noblest Blood, and of the most ancient and ample Patrimonies. I described that extraordinary Care always taken of their Education in Arts and Arms, to qualify them for being Counsellors born to the King and Kingdom; to 20
have a Share in the Legislature, to be Members of the highest Court of Judicature from whence there could be no Appeal; and to be Champions always ready for the Defence of their Prince and Country by their Valour, Conduct and Fidelity. That these were the Ornament and Bulwark of the Kingdom; worthy Followers of their most renowned Ancestors, whose Honour had been the Reward of their Virtue; from which their Posterity were never once known to degenerate. To these were joined several holy Persons, as part of that Assembly, under the Title of Bishops; whose peculiar Busi- 30
ness it is, to take care of Religion, and of those who instruct the People therein. These were searched and sought out through the whole Nation, by the Prince and wisest Counsellors, among such of the Priesthood, as were most deservedly distinguished by the Sanctity of their Lives, and the Depth

of their Erudition; who were indeed the spiritual Fathers of the Clergy and the People.

That, the other Part of the Parliament consisted of an Assembly called the House of Commons; who were all principal Gentlemen, *freely* picked and culled out by the People themselves, for their great Abilities, and Love of their Country, to represent the Wisdom of the whole Nation. And, these two Bodies make up the most august Assembly in *Europe*; to whom, in Conjunction with the Prince, the
10 whole Legislature is committed.

I then descended to the Courts of Justice, over which the Judges, those venerable Sages and Interpreters of the Law, presided, for determining the disputed Rights and Properties of Men, as well as for the Punishment of Vice, and Protection of Innocence. I mentioned the prudent Management of our Treasury; the Valour and Atchievements of our Forces by Sea and Land. I computed the Number of our People, by reckoning how many Millions there might be of each Religious Sect, or Political Party among us. I did not omit
20 even our Sports and Pastimes, or any other Particular which I thought might redound to the Honour of my Country. And, I finished all with a brief historical Account of Affairs and Events in *England* for about an hundred Years past.

This Conversation was not ended under five Audiences, each of several Hours; and the King heard the whole with great Attention; frequently taking Notes of what I spoke, as well as Memorandums of what Questions he intended to ask me.

When I had put an End to these long Discourses, his
30 Majesty in a sixth Audience consulting his Notes, proposed many Doubts, Queries, and Objections, upon every Article. He asked, what Methods were used to cultivate the Minds and Bodies of our young Nobility; and in what kind of Business they commonly spent the first and teachable Part of their Lives. What Course was taken to supply that Assembly,

when any noble Family became extinct. What Qualifications were necessary in those who are to be created new Lords: Whether the Humour of the Prince, a Sum of Money to a Court-Lady, or a Prime Minister; or a Design of strengthening a Party opposite to the publick Interest, ever happened to be Motives in those Advancements. What Share of Knowledge these Lords had in the Laws of their Country, and how they came by it, so as to enable them to decide the Properties of their Fellow-Subjects in the last Resort. Whether they were always so free from Avarice, Partialities, or Want, that a Bribe, or some other sinister View, could have no Place among them. Whether those holy Lords I spoke of, were constantly promoted to that Rank upon Account of their Knowledge in religious Matters, and the Sanctity of their Lives, had never been Compliers with the Times, while they were common Priests; or slavish prostitute Chaplains to some Nobleman, whose Opinions they continued servilely to follow after they were admitted into that Assembly.

He then desired to know, what Arts were practised in electing those whom I called Commoners. Whether, a Stranger with a strong Purse might not influence the vulgar Voters to chuse him before their own Landlord, or the most considerable Gentleman in the Neighbourhood. How it came to pass, that People were so violently bent upon getting into this Assembly, which I allowed to be a great Trouble and Expence, often to the Ruin of their Families, without any Salary or Pension: Because this appeared such an exalted Strain of Virtue and publick Spirit, that his Majesty seemed to doubt it might possibly not be always sincere: And he desired to know, whether such zealous Gentlemen could have any Views of refunding themselves for the Charges and Trouble they were at, by sacrificing the publick Good to the Designs of a weak and vicious Prince, in Conjunction with a corrupted Ministry. He multiplied his Questions, and sifted me thoroughly upon every Part of this Head; proposing numberless Enquiries and Objections, which I think it not prudent or convenient to repeat.

Upon what I said in relation to our Courts of Justice, his Majesty desired to be satisfied in several Points: And, this I was the better able to do, having been formerly almost ruined by a long Suit in Chancery, which was decreed for me with Costs. He asked, what Time was usually spent in determining between Right and Wrong; and what Degree of Expence. Whether Advocates and Orators had Liberty to plead in Causes manifestly known to be unjust, vexatious, or oppressive. Whether Party in Religion or Politicks were observed to be of any Weight in the Scale of Justice. Whether those pleading Orators were Persons educated in the general Knowledge of Equity; or only in provincial, national, and other local Customs. Whether they or their Judges had any Part in penning those Laws, which they assumed the Liberty of interpreting and glossing upon at their Pleasure. Whether they had ever at different Times pleaded for and against the same Cause, and cited Precedents to prove contrary Opinions. Whether they were a rich or a poor Corporation. Whether they received any pecuniary Reward for pleading or delivering their Opinions. And particularly whether they were ever admitted as Members in the lower Senate.

He fell next upon the Management of our Treasury; and said, he thought my Memory had failed me, because I computed our Taxes at about five or six Millions a Year; and when I came to mention the Issues, he found they sometimes amounted to more than double; for, the Notes he had taken were very particular in this Point; because he hoped, as he told me, that the Knowledge of our Conduct might be useful to him; and he could not be deceived in his Calculations. But, if what I told him were true, he was still at a Loss how a Kingdom could run out of its Estate like a private

Person. He asked me, who were our Creditors? and, where we found Money to pay them? He wondered to hear me talk of such chargeable and extensive Wars; that, certainly we must be a quarrelsome People, or live among very bad Neighbours; and that our Generals must needs be richer than our Kings. He asked, what Business we had out of our own Islands, unless upon the Score of Trade or Treaty, or to defend the Coasts with our Fleet. Above all, he was amazed to hear me talk of a mercenary standing Army in the Midst of Peace, and among a free People. He said, if we were 10 governed by our own Consent in the Persons of our Representatives, he could not imagine of whom we were afraid, or against whom we were to fight; and would hear my Opinion, whether a private Man's House might not better be defended by himself, his Children, and Family; than by half a Dozen Rascals picked up at a Venture in the Streets, for small Wages, who might get an Hundred Times more by cutting their Throats.

He laughed at my odd Kind of Arithmetick (as he was pleased to call it) in reckoning the Numbers of our People 20 by a Computation drawn from the several Sects among us in Religion and Politicks. He said, he knew no Reason, why those who entertain Opinions prejudicial to the Publick, should be obliged to change, or should not be obliged to conceal them. And, as it was Tyranny in any Government to require the first, so it was Weakness not to enforce the second: For, a Man may be allowed to keep Poisons in his Closet, but not to vend them about as Cordials.

He observed, that among the Diversions of our Nobility and Gentry, I had mentioned Gaming. He desired to know 30 at what Age this Entertainment was usually taken up, and when it was laid down. How much of their Time it employed; whether it ever went so high as to affect their Fortunes. Whether mean vicious People, by their Dexterity in that Art, might not arrive at great Riches, and sometimes keep our very Nobles in Dependance, as well as habituate them to vile Companions; wholly take them from the Improvement of their Minds, and force them by the Losses they received, to learn and practice that infamous Dexterity upon others.

He was perfectly astonished with the historical Account I gave him of our Affairs during the last Century; protesting it was only an Heap of Conspiracies, Rebellions, Murders, Massacres, Revolutions, Banishments; the very worst Effects that Avarice, Faction, Hypocrisy, Perfidiousness, Cruelty, Rage, Madness, Hatred, Envy, Lust, Malice, and Ambition could produce.

His Majesty in another Audience, was at the Pains to recapitulate the Sum of all I had spoken; compared the Questions he made, with the Answers I had given; then taking me into his Hands, and stroaking me gently, delivered himself in these Words, which I shall never forget, nor the Manner he spoke them in. My little Friend *Grildrig*; you have made a most admirable Panegyrick upon your Country. You have clearly proved that Ignorance, Idleness, and Vice are the proper Ingredients for qualifying a Legislator. That Laws are best explained, interpreted, and applied by those whose Interest and Abilities lie in perverting, confounding, and eluding them. I observe among you some Lines of an Institution, which in its Original might have been tolerable; but these half erased, and the rest wholly blurred and blotted by Corruptions. It doth not appear from all you have said, how any one Perfection is required towards the Procurement of any one Station among you; much less that Men are ennobled on Account of their Virtue, that Priests are advanced for their Piety or Learning, Soldiers for their Conduct or Valour, Judges for their Integrity, Senators for the Love of their Country, or Counsellors for their Wisdom. As for yourself (continued the King) who have spent the greatest Part of your Life in travelling; I am well disposed to hope you may hitherto have escaped many Vices of your

Country. But, by what I have gathered from your own Relation, and the Answers I have with much Pains wringed and extorted from you; I cannot but conclude the Bulk of your Natives, to be the most pernicious Race of little odious Vermin that Nature ever suffered to crawl upon the Surface of the Earth.

Chapter VII

The Author's Love of his Country: He makes a Proposal of much Advantage to the King; which is rejected. The King's great Ignorance in Politicks. The Learning of that Country very imperfect and confined. Their Laws, and military Affairs, and Parties in the State. 10

NOTHING but an extreme Love of Truth could have hindered me from concealing this Part of my Story. It was in vain to discover my Resentments, which were always turned into Ridicule: And I was forced to rest with Patience, while my noble and most beloved Country was so injuriously treated. I am heartily sorry as any of my Readers can possibly be, that such an Occasion was given: But this Prince happened to be so curious and inquisitive upon every Particular, that it could not consist either with Gratitude or good Manners to refuse giving him what Satisfaction I was able. Yet thus 20 much I may be allowed to say in my own Vindication; that I artfully eluded many of his Questions; and gave to every Point a more favourable turn by many Degrees than the strictness of Truth would allow. For, I have always born that laudable Partiality to my own Country, which *Dionysius Halicarnassensis* with so much Justice recommends to an Historian. I would hide the Frailties and Deformities of my Political Mother, and place her Virtues and Beauties in the most advantageous Light. This was my sincere Endeavour in those many Discourses I had with that Monarch, although 30 it unfortunately failed of Success.

But, great Allowances should be given to a King who lives wholly secluded from the rest of the World, and must therefore be altogether unacquainted with the Manners and

Customs that most prevail in other Nations: The want of which Knowledge will ever produce many *Prejudices*, and a certain *Narrowness of Thinking*; from which we and the politer Countries of *Europe* are wholly exempted. And it would be hard indeed, if so remote a Prince's Notions of Virtue and Vice were to be offered as a Standard for all Mankind.

To confirm what I have now said, and further to shew the miserable Effects of a *confined Education*; I shall here insert a Passage which will hardly obtain Belief. In hopes to ingra-
10 tiate my self farther into his Majesty's Favour, I told him of an Invention discovered between three and four hundred Years ago, to make a certain Powder; into an heap of which the smallest Spark of Fire falling, would kindle the whole in a Moment, although it were as big as a Mountain; and make it all fly up in the Air together, with a Noise and Agitation greater than Thunder. That, a proper Quantity of this Powder rammed into an hollow Tube of Brass or Iron, according to its Bigness, would drive a Ball of Iron or Lead with such Violence and Speed, as nothing was able to sustain
20 its Force. That, the largest Balls thus discharged, would not only Destroy whole Ranks of an Army at once; but batter the strongest Walls to the Ground; sink down Ships with a thousand Men in each, to the Bottom of the Sea; and when linked together by a Chain, would cut through Masts and Rigging; divide Hundreds of Bodies in the Middle, and lay all Waste before them. That we often put this Powder into large hollow Balls of Iron, and discharged them by an Engine into some City we were besieging; which would rip up the Pavement, tear the Houses to Pieces, burst and throw
30 Splinters on every Side, dashing out the Brains of all who came near. That I knew the Ingredients very well, which were Cheap, and common; I understood the Manner of compounding them, and could direct his Workmen how to make those Tubes of a Size proportionable to all other Things in his Majesty's Kingdom; and the largest need not be above

two hundred Foot long; twenty or thirty of which Tubes, charged with the proper Quantity of Powder and Balls, would batter down the Walls of the strongest Town in his Dominions in a few Hours; or destroy the whole Metropolis, if ever it should pretend to dispute his absolute Commands. This I humbly offered to his Majesty, as a small Tribute of Acknowledgment in return of so many Marks that I had received of his Royal Favour and Protection.

The King was struck with Horror at the Description I had given of those terrible Engines, and the Proposal I had made. 10 He was amazed how so impotent and groveling an Insect as I (these were his Expressions) could entertain such inhuman Ideas, and in so familiar a Manner as to appear wholly unmoved at all the Scenes of Blood and Desolation, which I had painted as the common Effects of those destructive Machines; whereof he said, some evil Genius, Enemy to Mankind, must have been the first Contriver. As for himself, he protested, that although few Things delighted him so much as new Discoveries in Art or in Nature; yet he would rather lose Half his Kingdom, than be privy to such a Secret; 20 which he commanded me, as I valued my Life, never to mention any more.

A strange Effect of *narrow Principles* and *short Views!* that a Prince possessed of every Quality which procures Veneration, Love and Esteem; of strong Parts, great Wisdom and profound Learning; endued with admirable Talents for Government, and almost adored by his Subjects; should from a *nice unnecessary Scruple,* whereof in *Europe* we can have no Conception, let slip an Opportunity put into his Hands, that would have made him absolute Master of the 30 Lives, the Liberties, and the Fortunes of his People. Neither do I say this with the least Intention to detract from the many Virtues of that excellent King; whose Character I am sensible will on this Account be very much lessened in the Opinion of an *English* Reader: But, I take this Defect

among them to have risen from their Ignorance; by not having hitherto reduced *Politicks* into a *Science,* as the more acute Wits of *Europe* have done. For, I remember very well, in a Discourse one Day with the King; when I happened to say, there were several thousand Books among us written upon the *Art of Government*; it gave him (directly contrary to my Intention) a very mean Opinion of our Understandings. He professed both to abominate and despise all *Mystery, Refinement,* and *Intrigue,* either in a Prince or a Minister.
10 He could not tell what I meant by *Secrets of State,* where an Enemy or some Rival Nation were not in the Case. He confined the Knowledge of governing within very *narrow Bounds*; to common Sense and Reason, to Justice and Lenity, to the Speedy Determination of Civil and criminal Causes; with some other obvious Topicks which are not worth considering. And, he gave it for his Opinion; that whoever could make two Ears of Corn, or two Blades of Grass to grow upon a Spot of Ground where only one grew before; would deserve better of Mankind, and do more essential Service to his
20 Country, than the whole Race of Politicians put together.

The Learning of this People is very defective; consisting only in Morality, History, Poetry and Mathematicks; wherein they must be allowed to excel. But, the last of these is wholly applied to what may be useful in Life; to the Improvement of Agriculture and all mechanical Arts; so that among us it would be little esteemed. And as to Ideas, Entities, Abstractions and Transcendentals, I could never drive the least Conception into their Heads.

No Law of that Country must exceed in Words the Num-
30 ber of Letters in their Alphabet; which consists only of two and twenty. But indeed, few of them extend even to that Length. They are expressed in the most plain and simple Terms, wherein those People are not Mercurial enough to discover above one Interpretation. And, to write a Comment upon any Law, is a capital Crime. As to the Decision of civil

Causes, or Proceedings against Criminals, their Precedents are so few, that they have little Reason to boast of any extraordinary Skill in either.

They have had the Art of Printing, as well as the *Chinese*, Time out of Mind. But their Libraries are not very large; for that of the King's, which is reckoned the largest, doth not amount to above a thousand Volumes; placed in a Gallery of twelve hundred Foot long; from whence I had Liberty to borrow what Books I pleased. The Queen's Joyner had contrived in one of *Glumdalclitch*'s Rooms a Kind of wooden 10 Machine five and twenty Foot high, formed like a standing Ladder; the Steps were each fifty Foot long: It was indeed a moveable Pair of Stairs, the lowest End placed at ten Foot Distance from the Wall of the Chamber. The Book I had a Mind to read was put up leaning against the Wall. I first mounted to the upper Step of the Ladder, and turning my Face towards the Book, began at the Top of the Page, and so walking to the Right and Left about eight or ten Paces according to the Length of the Lines, till I had gotten a little below the Level of mine Eyes; and then descending gradu- 20 ally till I came to the Bottom: After which I mounted again, and began the other Page in the same Manner, and so turned over the Leaf, which I could easily do with both my Hands, for it was as thick and stiff as a Paste-board, and in the largest Folio's not above eighteen or twenty Foot long.

Their Stile is clear, masculine, and smooth, but not Florid; for they avoid nothing more than multiplying unnecessary Words, or using various Expressions. I have perused many of their Books, especially those in History and Morality. Among the latter I was much diverted with a little old 30 Treatise, which always lay in *Glumdalclitch*'s Bedchamber, and belonged to her Governess, a grave elderly Gentlewoman, who dealt in Writings of Morality and Devotion. The Book treats of the Weakness of Human kind; and is in little Esteem except among Women and the Vulgar. However, I was curious to see what an Author of that Country could say upon such a Subject. This Writer went through all the usual Topicks of *European* Moralists; shewing how diminutive, contemptible, and helpless an Animal was Man in his own Nature; how unable to defend himself from the Inclemencies of the Air, or the Fury of wild Beasts: How much he was excelled by one Creature in Strength, by another in Speed, by a third in Foresight, by a fourth in Industry. He added, that Nature was degenerated in these latter declining Ages of the World, and could now produce only small abortive Births in Comparison of those in ancient Times. He said, it was very reasonable to think, not only that the Species of Men were originally much larger, but also that there must have been Giants in former Ages; which, as it is asserted by History and Tradition, so it hath been confirmed by huge Bones and Sculls casually dug up in several Parts of the Kingdom, far exceeding the common dwindled Race of Man in our Days. He argued, that the very Laws of Nature absolutely required we should have been made in the Beginning, of a Size more large and robust, not so liable to Destruction from every little Accident of a Tile falling from an House, or a Stone cast from the Hand of a Boy, or of being drowned in a little Brook. From this Way of Reasoning the Author drew several moral Applications useful in the Conduct of Life, but needless here to repeat. For my own Part, I could not avoid reflecting, how universally this Talent was spread of drawing Lectures in Morality, or indeed rather Matter of Discontent and repining, from the Quarrels we raise with Nature. And, I believe upon a strict Enquiry, those Quarrels might be shewn as ill-grounded among us, as they are among that People.

As to their military Affairs; they boast that the King's Army consists of an hundred and seventy six thousand Foot, and thirty two thousand Horse: If that may be called an Army which is made up of Tradesmen in the several Cities, and Farmers in the Country, whose Commanders are only the Nobility and Gentry, without Pay or Reward. They are indeed perfect enough in their Exercises; and under very good Discipline, wherein I saw no great merit: For, how should it be otherwise, where every Farmer is under the Command of his own Landlord, and every Citizen under that of the principal Men in his own City, chosen after the Manner of *Venice* by *Ballot*?

I have often seen the Militia of *Lorbrulgrud* drawn out to Exercise in a great Field near the City, of twenty Miles 10 Square. They were in all not above twenty five thousand Foot, and six thousand Horse; but it was impossible for me to compute their Number, considering the Space of Ground they took up. A *Cavalier* mounted on a large Steed might be about Ninety Foot high. I have seen this whole Body of Horse upon the Word of Command draw their Swords at once, and brandish them in the Air. Imagination can Figure nothing so Grand, so surprising and so astonishing. It looked as if ten thousand Flashes of Lightning were darting at the same time from every Quarter of the Sky. 20

I was curious to know how this Prince, to whose Dominions there is no Access from any other Country, came to think of Armies, or to teach his People the Practice of military Discipline. But I was soon informed, both by Conversation, and Reading their Histories. For, in the Course of many Ages they have been troubled with the same Disease, to which the whole Race of Mankind is Subject; the Nobility often contending for Power, the People for Liberty, and the King for absolute Dominion. All which, however happily tempered by the Laws of that Kingdom, have been sometimes violated 30 by each of the three Parties; and have more than once occasioned Civil Wars, the last whereof was happily put an End to by this Prince's Grandfather in a general Composition; and the Militia then settled with common Consent hath been ever since kept in the strictest Duty.

Part III, Chapter 3

A Phænomenon solved by modern Philosophy and Astronomy. The Laputians *great Improvements in the latter. The King's Method of suppressing Insurrections.*

I DESIRED Leave of this Prince to see the Curiosities of the Island; which he was graciously pleased to grant, and ordered my Tutor to attend me. I chiefly wanted to know to what Cause in Art or in Nature, it owed its several Motions; whereof I will now give a philosophical Account to the Reader.

10 The flying or floating Island is exactly circular; its Diameter 7837 Yards, or about four Miles and an Half, and consequently contains ten Thousand Acres. It is three Hundred Yards thick. The Bottom, or under Surface, which appears to those who view it from below, is one even regular Plate of Adamant, shooting up to the Height of about two Hundred Yards. Above it lye the several Minerals in their usual Order; and over all is a Coat of rich Mould ten or twelve Foot deep. The Declivity of the upper Surface, from the Circumference to the Center, is the natural Cause why all the 20 Dews and Rains which fall upon the Island, are conveyed in small Rivulets towards the Middle, where they are emptyed into four large Basons, each of about Half a Mile in Circuit, and two Hundred Yards distant from the Center. From these Basons the Water is continually exhaled by the Sun in the Day-time, which effectually prevents their overflowing. Besides, as it is in the Power of the Monarch to raise the Island above the Region of Clouds and Vapours, he can prevent the falling of Dews and Rains whenever he pleases. For the highest Clouds cannot rise above two Miles, as 30 Naturalists agree, at least they were never known to do so in that Country.

At the Center of the Island there is a Chasm about fifty Yards in Diameter, from whence the Astronomers descend into a large Dome, which is therefore called *Flandona Gagnole*, or the *Astronomers Cave*; situated at the Depth of an Hundred Yards beneath the upper Surface of the Adamant. In this Cave are Twenty Lamps continually burning, which from the Reflection of the Adamant cast a strong Light into every Part. The Place is stored with great Variety of Sextants, Quadrants, Telescopes, Astrolabes, and other Astronomical Instruments. But the greatest Curiosity, upon which the Fate of the Island depends, is a Load-stone of a prodigious Size, in Shape resembling a Weaver's Shuttle. It 10 is in Length six Yards, and in the thickest Part at least three Yards over. This Magnet is sustained by a very strong Axle of Adamant, passing through its Middle, upon which it plays, and is poized so exactly that the weakest Hand can turn it. It is hooped round with an hollow Cylinder of Adamant, four Foot deep, as many thick, and twelve Yards in Diameter, placed horizontally, and supported by Eight Adamantine Feet, each Six Yards high. In the Middle of the Concave Side there is a Groove Twelve Inches deep, in which the Extremities of the Axle are lodged, and turned round as 20 there is Occasion.

This Stone cannot be moved from its Place by any Force, because the Hoop and its Feet are one continued Piece with that Body of Adamant which constitutes the Bottom of the Island. By Means of this Load-stone, the Island is made to rise and fall, and move from one Place to another. For, with respect to that Part of the Earth over which the Monarch presides, the Stone is endued at one of its Sides with an attractive Power, and at the other with a repulsive. Upon placing the Magnet erect with its attracting End towards the Earth, the 30 Island descends; but when the repelling Extremity points downwards, the Island mounts directly upwards. When the Position of the Stone is oblique, the Motion of the Island is so too. For in this Magnet the Forces always act in Lines parallel to its Direction.

By this oblique Motion the Island is conveyed to different Parts of the Monarch's Dominions. To explain the Manner of its Progress, let *A B* represent a Line drawn cross the Dominions of *Balnibarbi*; let the Line *c d* represent the Load-stone, of which let *d* be the repelling End, and *c* the attracting End, the Island being over *C*; let the Stone be placed in the Position *c d* with its repelling End downwards; then the Island will be driven upwards obliquely towards *D*. When it is arrived at *D*, let the Stone be turned upon
10 its Axle till its attracting End points towards *E*, and then the Island will be carried obliquely towards *E*; where if the Stone be again turned upon its Axle till it stands in the Position *E F*, with its repelling Point downwards, the Island will rise obliquely towards *F*, where by directing the attracting End towards *G*, the Island may be carried to *G*, and from *G* to *H*, by turning the Stone, so as to make its repelling Extremity point directly downwards. And thus by changing the Situation of the Stone as often as there is Occasion, the Island is made to rise and fall by Turns in an oblique Direc-
20 tion; and by those alternate Risings and Fallings (the Obliquity being not considerable) is conveyed from one Part of the Dominions to the other.

But it must be observed, that this Island cannot move beyond the Extent of the Dominions below; nor can it rise above the Height of four Miles. For which the Astronomers (who have written large Systems concerning the Stone) assign the following Reason: That the Magnetick Virtue does not extend beyond the Distance of four Miles, and that the Mineral which acts upon the Stone in the Bowels of
30 the Earth, and in the Sea about six Leagues distant from the Shoar, is not diffused through the whole Globe, but terminated with the Limits of the King's Dominions: And it was easy from the great Advantage of such a superior Situation, for a Prince to bring under his Obedience whatever Country lay within the Attraction of that Magnet.

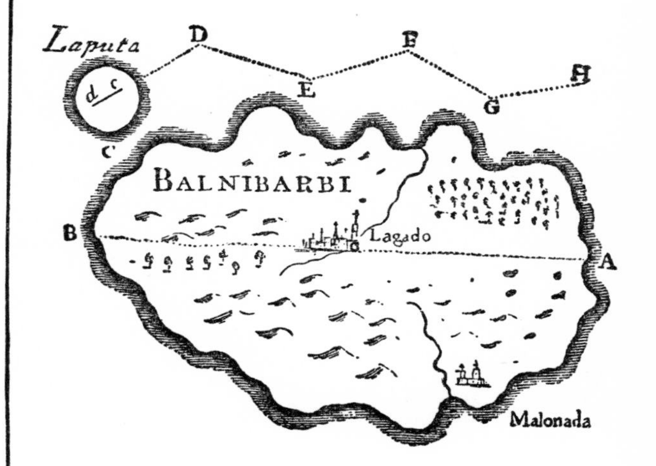
Laputa
d c
D
E
F
G
H
C
BALNIBARBI
B
Lagado
A
Malonada

When the Stone is put parallel to the Plane of the Horizon, the Island standeth still; for in that Case, the Extremities of it being at equal Distance from the Earth, act with equal Force, the one in drawing downwards, the other in pushing upwards; and consequently no Motion can ensue.

This Load-stone is under the Care of certain Astronomers, who from Time to Time give it such Positions as the Monarch directs. They spend the greatest Part of their Lives in observing the celestial Bodies, which they do by the Assistance of Glasses, far excelling ours in Goodness. For, although their largest Telescopes do not exceed three Feet, they magnify much more than those of a Hundred with us, and shew the Stars with greater Clearness. This Advantage hath enabled them to extend their Discoveries much farther than our Astronomers in *Europe*. They have made a Catalogue of ten Thousand fixed Stars, whereas the largest of ours do not contain above one third Part of that Number. They have likewise discovered two lesser Stars, or *Satellites*, which revolve about *Mars*; whereof the innermost is distant from the Center of the primary Planet exactly three of his Diameters, and the outermost five; the former revolves in the Space of ten Hours, and the latter in Twenty-one and an Half; so that the Squares of their periodical Times, are very near in the same Proportion with the Cubes of their Distance from the Center of *Mars*; which evidently shews them to be governed by the same Law of Gravitation, that influences the other heavenly Bodies.

They have observed Ninety-three different Comets, and settled their Periods with great Exactness. If this be true, (and they affirm it with great Confidence) it is much to be wished that their Observations were made publick; whereby the Theory of Comets, which at present is very lame and defective, might be brought to the same Perfection with other Parts of Astronomy.

The King would be the most absolute Prince in the Universe, if he could but prevail on a Ministry to join with him; but these having their Estates below on the Continent, and considering that the Office of a Favourite hath a very uncertain Tenure, would never consent to the enslaving their Country.

If any Town should engage in Rebellion or Mutiny, fall into violent Factions, or refuse to pay the usual Tribute; the King hath two Methods of reducing them to Obedience. The 10 first and the mildest Course is by keeping the Island hovering over such a Town, and the Lands about it; whereby he can deprive them of the Benefit of the Sun and the Rain, and consequently afflict the Inhabitants with Dearth and Diseases. And if the Crime deserve it, they are at the same time pelted from above with great Stones, against which they have no Defence, but by creeping into Cellars or Caves, while the Roofs of their Houses are beaten to Pieces. But if they still continue obstinate, or offer to raise Insurrections; he proceeds to the last Remedy, by letting the Island drop 20 directly upon their Heads, which makes a universal Destruction both of Houses and Men. However, this is an Extremity to which the Prince is seldom driven, neither indeed is he willing to put it in Execution; nor dare his Ministers advise him to an Action, which as it would render them odious to the People, so it would be a great Damage to their own Estates that lie all below; for the Island is the King's Demesn.

But there is still indeed a more weighty Reason, why the Kings of this Country have been always averse from executing so terrible an Action, unless upon the utmost Necessity. 30 For if the Town intended to be destroyed should have in it any tall Rocks, as it generally falls out in the larger Cities; a Situation probably chosen at first with a View to prevent such a Catastrophe: Or if it abound in high Spires or Pillars of Stone, a sudden Fall might endanger the Bottom or under Surface of the Island, which although it consist as I have said, of one entire Adamant two hundred Yards thick, might happen to crack by too great a Choque, or burst by approaching too near the Fires from the Houses below; as the Backs both of Iron and Stone will often do in our Chimneys. Of all this the People are well apprized, and understand how far to carry their Obstinacy, where their Liberty or Property is concerned. And the King, when he is highest provoked, and most determined to press a City to Rubbish, orders the Island to descend with great Gentleness, out of a Pretence of Tenderness to his People, but indeed for fear of 10 breaking the Adamantine Bottom; in which Case it is the Opinion of all their Philosophers, that the Load-stone could no longer hold it up, and the whole Mass would fall to the Ground.

By a fundamental Law of this Realm, neither the King nor either of his two elder Sons, are permitted to leave the Island; nor the Queen till she is past Child-bearing.

Part IV, Chapter 10

The Author's Oeconomy, and happy Life among the Houyhnhnms. *His great Improvement in Virtue, by conversing with them. Their Conversations. The Author hath Notice given him by his Master that he must depart from the Country. He falls into a Swoon for Grief, but sub-* 20 *mits. He contrives and finishes a Canoo, by the Help of a Fellow-Servant, and puts to Sea at a Venture.*

I HAD settled my little Oeconomy to my own Heart's Content. My Master had ordered a Room to be made for me after their Manner, about six Yards from the House; the Sides and Floors of which I plaistered with Clay, and covered with Rush-mats of my own contriving: I had beaten Hemp, which there grows wild, and made of it a Sort of Ticking: This I filled with the Feathers of several Birds I had taken with Springes made of *Yahoos* Hairs; and were excel- 30 lent Food. I had worked two Chairs with my Knife, the Sorrel Nag helping me in the grosser and more laborious

Part. When my Cloaths were worn to Rags, I made my self others with the Skins of Rabbets, and of a certain beautiful Animal about the same Size, called *Nnuhnoh,* the Skin of which is covered with a fine Down. Of these I likewise made very tolerable Stockings. I soaled my Shoes with Wood which I cut from a Tree, and fitted to the upper Leather, and when this was worn out, I supplied it with the Skins of *Yahoos,* dried in the Sun. I often got Honey out of hollow Trees, which I mingled with Water, or eat it with my Bread.
10 No Man could more verify the Truth of these two Maxims, *That, Nature is very easily satisfied*; and, *That, Necessity is the Mother of Invention.* I enjoyed perfect Health of Body, and Tranquility of Mind; I did not feel the Treachery or Inconstancy of a Friend, nor the Injuries of a secret or open Enemy. I had no Occasion of bribing, flattering or pimping, to procure the Favour of any great Man, or of his Minion. I wanted no Fence against Fraud or Oppression: Here was neither Physician to destroy my Body, nor Lawyer to ruin my Fortune: No Informer to watch my Words and Actions,
20 or forge Accusations against me for Hire: Here were no Gibers, Censurers, Backbiters, Pickpockets, Highwaymen, House-breakers, Attorneys, Bawds, Buffoons, Gamesters, Politicians, Wits, Spleneticks, tedious Talkers, Controvertists, Ravishers, Murderers, Robbers, Virtuoso's; no Leaders or Followers of Party and Faction; no Encouragers to Vice, by Seducement or Examples: No Dungeon, Axes, Gibbets, Whipping-posts, or Pillories; No cheating Shopkeepers or Mechanicks: No Pride, Vanity or Affectation: No Fops, Bullies, Drunkards, strolling Whores, or Poxes: No ranting,
30 lewd, expensive Wives: No stupid, proud Pedants: No importunate, over-bearing, quarrelsome, noisy, roaring, empty, conceited, swearing Companions: No Scoundrels raised from the Dust upon the Merit of their Vices; or Nobility thrown into it on account of their Virtues: No Lords, Fidlers, Judges or Dancing-masters.

I had the Favour of being admitted to several *Houyhnhnms*, who came to visit or dine with my Master; where his Honour graciously suffered me to wait in the Room, and listen to their Discourse. Both he and his Company would often descend to ask me Questions, and receive my Answers. I had also sometimes the Honour of attending my Master in his Visits to others. I never presumed to speak, except in answer to a Question; and then I did it with inward Regret, because it was a Loss of so much Time for improving my self: But I was infinitely delighted with the Station of an humble 10 Auditor in such Conversations, where nothing passed but what was useful, expressed in the fewest and most significant Words: Where (as I have already said) the greatest *Decency* was observed, without the least Degree of Ceremony; where no Person spoke without being pleased himself, and pleasing his Companions: Where there was no Interruption, Tediousness, Heat, or Difference of Sentiments. They have a Notion, That when People are met together, a short Silence doth much improve Conversation: This I found to be true; for during those little Intermissions of Talk, new Ideas would 20 arise in their Minds, which very much enlivened the Discourse. Their Subjects are generally on Friendship and Benevolence; on Order and Oeconomy; sometimes upon the visible Operations of Nature, or ancient Traditions; upon the Bounds and Limits of Virtue; upon the unerring Rules of Reason; or upon some Determinations, to be taken at the next great Assembly; and often upon the various Excellencies of *Poetry*. I may add, without Vanity, that my Presence often gave them sufficient Matter for Discourse, because it afforded my Master an Occasion of letting his 30 Friends into the History of me and my Country, upon which they were all pleased to discant in a Manner not very advantageous to human Kind; and for that Reason I shall not repeat what they said: Only I may be allowed to observe, That his Honour, to my great Admiration, appeared to understand the Nature of *Yahoos* much better than my self. He went through all our Vices and Follies, and discovered many which I had never mentioned to him; by only supposing what Qualities a *Yahoo* of their Country, with a small Proportion of Reason, might be capable of exerting: And concluded, with too much Probability, how vile as well as miserable such a Creature must be.

I freely confess, that all the little Knowledge I have of any Value, was acquired by the Lectures I received from my Master, and from hearing the Discourses of him and his Friends; to which I should be prouder to listen, than to dictate to the greatest and wisest Assembly in *Europe*. I admired the Strength, Comeliness and Speed of the Inhabitants; and such a Constellation of Virtues in such amiable Persons produced in me the highest Veneration. At first, indeed, I did not feel that natural Awe which the *Yahoos* and all other Animals bear towards them; but it grew upon me by Degrees, much sooner than I imagined, and was mingled with a respectful Love and Gratitude, that they would condescend to distinguish me from the rest of my Species.

When I thought of my Family, my Friends, my Countrymen, or human Race in general, I considered them as they really were, *Yahoos* in Shape and Disposition, perhaps a little more civilized, and qualified with the Gift of Speech; but making no other Use of Reason, than to improve and multiply those Vices, whereof their Brethren in this Country had only the Share that Nature allotted them. When I happened to behold the Reflection of my own Form in a Lake or Fountain, I turned away my Face in Horror and detestation of my self; and could better endure the Sight of a common *Yahoo*, than of my own Person. By conversing with the *Houyhnhnms*, and looking upon them with Delight, I fell to imitate their Gait and Gesture, which is now grown into a Habit; and my Friends often tell me in a blunt Way, that *I trot like a Horse*; which, however, I take for a great

Compliment: Neither shall I disown, that in speaking I am apt to fall into the Voice and manner of the *Houyhnhnms*, and hear my self ridiculed on that Account without the least Mortification.

In the Midst of this Happiness, when I looked upon my self to be fully settled for Life, my Master sent for me one Morning a little earlier than his usual Hour. I observed by his Countenance that he was in some Perplexity, and at a Loss how to begin what he had to speak. After a short Silence, he told me, he did not know how I would take what he was 10 going to say: That, in the last general Assembly, when the Affair of the *Yahoos* was entered upon, the Representatives had taken Offence at his keeping a *Yahoo* (meaning my self) in his Family more like a *Houyhnhnm* than a Brute Animal. That, he was known frequently to converse with me, as if he could receive some Advantage or Pleasure in my Company: That, such a Practice was not agreeable to Reason or Nature, nor a thing ever heard of before among them. The Assembly did therefore *exhort* him, either to employ me like the rest of my Species, or command me to swim back to the 20 Place from whence I came. That, the first of these Expedients was utterly rejected by all the *Houyhnhnms*, who had ever seen me at his House or their own: For, they alledged, That because I had some Rudiments of Reason, added to the natural Pravity of those Animals, it was to be feared, I might be able to seduce them into the woody and mountainous Parts of the Country, and bring them in Troops by Night to destroy the *Houyhnhnms* Cattle, as being naturally of the ravenous Kind, and averse from Labour.

My Master added, That he was daily pressed by the 30 *Houyhnhnms* of the Neighbourhood to have the Assembly's *Exhortation* executed, which he could not put off much longer. He doubted, it would be impossible for me to swim to another Country; and therefore wished I would contrive some Sort of Vehicle resembling those I had described to him, that might carry me on the Sea; in which Work I should have the Assistance of his own Servants, as well as those of his Neighbours. He concluded, that for his own Part he could have been content to keep me in his Service as long as I lived; because he found I had cured myself of some bad Habits and Dispositions, by endeavouring, as far as my inferior Nature was capable, to imitate the *Houyhnhnms*.

I should here observe to the Reader, that a Decree of the 10 general Assembly in this Country, is expressed by the Word *Hnhloayn*, which signifies an *Exhortation*; as near as I can render it: For they have no Conception how a rational Creature can be *compelled*, but only advised, or *exhorted*; because no Person can disobey Reason, without giving up his Claim to be a rational Creature.

I was struck with the utmost Grief and Despair at my Master's Discourse; and being unable to support the Agonies I was under, I fell into a Swoon at his Feet: When I came to myself, he told me, that he concluded I had been dead. 20 (For these People are subject to no such Imbecillities of Nature) I answered, in a faint Voice, that Death would have been too great an Happiness; that although I could not blame the Assembly's *Exhortation*, or the Urgency of his Friends; yet in my weak and corrupt Judgment, I thought it might consist with Reason to have been less rigorous. That, I could not swim a League, and probably the nearest Land to theirs might be distant above an Hundred: That, many Materials, necessary for making a small Vessel to carry me off, were wholly wanting in this Country, which 30 however, I would attempt in Obedience and Gratitude to his Honour, although I concluded the thing to be impossible, and therefore looked on myself as already devoted to Destruction. That, the certain Prospect of an unnatural Death, was the least of my Evils: For, supposing I should escape with Life by some strange Adventure, how could I think with Temper, of passing my Days among *Yahoos*, and relapsing into my old Corruptions, for want of Examples to lead and keep me within the Paths of Virtue. That, I knew too well upon what solid Reasons all the Determinations of the wise *Houyhnhnms* were founded, not to be shaken by Arguments of mine, a miserable *Yahoo*; and therefore after presenting him with my humble Thanks for the Offer of his Servants Assistance in making a Vessel, and desiring a reasonable Time for so difficult a Work, I told him, I would endeavour to preserve a wretched Being; and, if ever I returned to *England*, was not without Hopes of being useful to my own Species, by celebrating the Praises of the renowned *Houyhnhnms*, and proposing their Virtues to the Imitation of Mankind.

My Master in a few Words made me a very gracious Reply, allowed me the Space of two *Months* to finish my Boat; and ordered the Sorrel Nag, my Fellow-Servant, (for so at this Distance I may presume to call him) to follow my Instructions, because I told my Master, that his Help would be sufficient, and I knew he had a Tenderness for me.

In his Company my first Business was to go to that Part of the Coast, where my rebellious Crew had ordered me to be set on Shore. I got upon a Height, and looking on every Side into the Sea, fancied I saw a small Island, towards the *North-East*: I took out my Pocket-glass, and could then clearly distinguish it about five Leagues off, as I computed; but it appeared to the Sorrel Nag to be only a blue Cloud: For, as he had no Conception of any Country beside his own, so he could not be as expert in distinguishing remote Objects at Sea, as we who so much converse in that Element.

After I had discovered this Island, I considered no farther; but resolved, it should, if possible, be the first Place of my Banishment, leaving the Consequence to Fortune.

I returned home, and consulting with the Sorrel Nag, we went into a Copse at some Distance, where I with my Knife, and he with a sharp Flint fastened very artificially, after their Manner, to a wooden Handle, cut down several Oak Wattles about the Thickness of a Walking-staff, and some larger Pieces. But I shall not trouble the Reader with a particular Description of my own Mechanicks: Let it suffice to say, that in six Weeks time, with the Help of the Sorrel Nag, who performed the Parts that required most Labour, I finished a Sort of *Indian* Canoo, but much larger, covering it with the Skins of *Yahoos*, well stitched together, with 10 hempen Threads of my own making. My Sail was likewise composed of the Skins of the same Animal; but I made use of the youngest I could get, the older being too tough and thick; and I likewise provided myself with four Paddles. I laid in a Stock of boiled Flesh, of Rabbets and Fowls; and took with me two Vessels, one filled with Milk, and the other with Water.

I tried my Canoo in a large Pond near my Master's House, and then corrected in it what was amiss; stopping all the Chinks with *Yahoos* Tallow, till I found it stanch, and able 20 to bear me, and my Freight. And when it was as compleat as I could possibly make it, I had it drawn on a Carriage very gently by *Yahoos*, to the Sea-side, under the Conduct of the Sorrel Nag, and another Servant.

When all was ready, and the Day came for my Departure, I took Leave of my Master and Lady, and the whole Family, mine Eyes flowing with Tears, and my Heart quite sunk with Grief. But his Honour, out of Curiosity, and perhaps (if I may speak it without Vanity) partly out of Kindness, was determined to see me in my Canoo; and got several of 30 his neighbouring Friends to accompany him. I was forced to wait above an Hour for the Tide, and then observing the Wind very fortunately bearing towards the Island, to which I intended to steer my Course, I took a second Leave of my Master: But as I was going to prostrate myself to kiss his Hoof, he did me the Honour to raise it gently to my Mouth.

I am not ignorant how much I have been censured for mentioning this last Particular. Detractors are pleased to think it improbable, that so illustrious a Person should descend to give so great a Mark of Distinction to a Creature so inferior as I. Neither have I forgot, how apt some Travellers are to boast of extraordinary Favours they have received. But, if these Censurers were better acquainted with the noble and courteous Disposition of the *Houyhnhnms,* they would soon change their Opinion.

I paid my Respects to the rest of the *Houyhnhnms* in his 10 Honour's Company; then getting into my Canoo, I pushed off from Shore.

THE INTELLIGENCER

Number III (1728)

A Vindication of Mr. Gay, and the Beggar's Opera

Ipse per omnes
Ibit personas, & turbam reddet in unam.

The *Players* having now almost done with the Comedy, called the *Beggars Opera* for the Season; it may be no unpleasant Speculation, to reflect a little upon this *Dramatick Piece,* so singular in the Subject and Manner, so much an Original, and which hath frequently given so very agreeable an Entertainment.

Although an evil *Taste* be very apt to prevail, both here and in *London*; yet there is a Point, which whoever can rightly touch, will never fail of pleasing a very great 10 Majority; so great, that the Dislikers, out of Dulness or Affectation, will be silent, and forced to fall in with the Herd: The Point I mean, is what we call *Humour*; which, in its Perfection, is allowed to be much preferable to *Wit*; if it be not rather the most useful, and agreeable Species of it.

I agree with Sir *William Temple,* that the Word is peculiar to our *English Tongue*; but I differ from him in the Opinion, that the Thing it self is peculiar to the *English Nation,* because the contrary may be found in many *Spanish, Italian* and *French* Productions; and particularly, whoever hath a *Taste* for *True* 20 *Humour,* will find a hundred Instances of it in those Volumes printed in *France,* under the Name of *Le Theatre Italien*; to say nothing of *Rabelais, Cervantes,* and many others.

Now I take the *Comedy* or *Farce,* (or whatever Name the *Criticks* will allow it) called the *Beggars Opera,* to excel in this Article of *Humour*; and upon that Merit to have met with such prodigious Success both here and in *England.*

As to *Poetry, Eloquence* and *Musick,* which are said to have most Power over the Minds of Men, it is certain that very few have a *Taste* or *Judgment* of the Excellencies of the two former; and if a Man succeed in either, it is upon the Authority of those *few Judges,* that lend their *Taste* to the Bulk of Readers, who have none of their own. I am told there are as few good Judges in *Musick*; and that among those who crowd the *Opera's,* Nine in Ten go thither merely out of *Curiosity, Fashion,* or *Affectation.*

But a *Taste* for *Humour* is in some Manner fixed to the very Nature of Man, and generally obvious to the Vulgar, except upon Subjects too refined, and superior to their Understanding. 10

And, as this *Taste* of *Humour* is purely natural, so is *Humour* it self; neither is it a *Talent* confined to Men of *Wit,* or *Learning*; for we observe it sometimes among common Servants, and the Meanest of the People, while the very Owners are often ignorant of the Gift they possess.

I know very well, that this happy *Talent* is contemptibly treated by *Criticks,* under the Name of *low Humour,* or *low Comedy*; but I know likewise, that the *Spaniards* and *Italians,* who are allowed to have the most Wit of any *Nation* in *Europe,* do most excel in it, and do most esteem it. 20

By what Disposition of the Mind, what Influence of the Stars, or what Situation of the *Climate* this Endowment is bestowed upon Mankind, may be a Question fit for *Philosophers* to discuss. It is certainly the best Ingredient towards that Kind of Satyr, which is most useful, and give the least Offence; which, instead of lashing, laughs Men out of their Follies, and Vices; and is the Character which gives *Horace* the Preference to *Juvenal.* 30

And, although some Things are too serious, solemn, or sacred to be turned into Ridicule, yet the Abuses of them are certainly not; since it is allowed that Corruption in *Religion, Politics,* and *Law,* may be proper *Topicks* for this kind of *Satyr.*

There are two Ends that Men propose in writing Satyr; one of them less Noble than the other, as regarding nothing further than the private Satisfaction, and Pleasure of the Writer; but without any View towards *Personal Malice*: the other is a *Publick Spirit*, prompting Men of *Genius* and Virtue, to mend the World as far as they are able. And as both these Ends are innocent, so the latter is highly commendable. With Regard to the former, I demand, whether I have not as good a Title to laugh, as Men have to be 10 ridiculous; and to expose Vice, as another hath to be vicious. If I ridicule the Follies and Corruptions of a *Court*, a *Ministry*, or a *Senate*, are they not amply paid by *Pensions*, *Titles*, and *Power*; while I expect and desire no other Reward, than that of laughing with a few Friends in a Corner? Yet, if those who take Offence, think me in the Wrong, I am ready to change the Scene with them, whenever they please.

But if my Design be to make Mankind better, then I think it is my Duty; at least I am sure it is the Interest of those very *Courts* and *Ministers*, whose Follies or Vices 20 I ridicule, to reward me for my good Intentions: For if it be reckoned a high Point of Wisdom to get the Laughers on our Side; it is much more easy, as well as wise, to get those on our Side, who can make Millions laugh when they please.

A Modest Proposal for Preventing the Children of Ireland from being a Burden to their Parents or Country and for making them beneficial to the Publick (*1729*)

IT is a melancholly Object to those, who walk through this great Town or travel in the Country, when they see the *Streets*, the *Roads* and *Cabbin-doors* crowded with *Beggars* of the Female Sex, followed by three, four, or six Children, *all in Rags*, and importuning every Passenger for an Alms. These *Mothers* instead of being able to work for their honest Livelyhood, are forced to employ all their Time in stroling to beg Sustenance for their *helpless Infants*, who, as they grow up, either turn *Thieves* for want of Work; or leave *their dear Native Country, to fight for the Pretender in* Spain; or sell themselves to the *Barbadoes*.

I think it is agreed by all Parties, that this prodigious number of Children in the Arms, or on the Backs, or at the *Heels* of their *Mothers*, and frequently of their *Fathers*, is *in* 10 *the present deplorable state of the Kingdom*, a very great additional Grievance; and therefore, whoever could find out a fair, cheap and easy Method of making these Children sound and useful Members of the Common-wealth, would deserve so well of the Publick, as to have his Statue set up for a Preserver of the Nation.

But my Intention is very far from being confined to provide only for the Children of *professed Beggars*: it is of a much greater Extent, and shall take in the whole Number of Infants at a certain Age, who are born of Parents in effect as little able to 20 support them, as those who demand our Charity in the Streets.

As to my own Part, having turned my Thoughts, for many Years, upon this important Subject, and maturely weighed the several *Schemes of other Projectors*, I have always found them grosly mistaken in their *computation*. It is true a Child, *just dropt from its Dam*, may be supported by her Milk, for a Solar Year with little other Nourishment at most not above the Value of two Shillings, which the Mother may certainly get, or the Value in *Scraps*, by *her lawful Occupation of Begging*; and it is exactly at one Year Old that 30 I propose to provide for them in such a Manner, as, instead of being a *Charge* upon their *Parents*, or the *Parish*, or *wanting Food and Raiment* for the rest of their Lives, they shall, on the Contrary, contribute to the *Feeding* and partly to the *Cloathing* of many Thousands.

There is likewise another great Advantage in my Scheme, that it will prevent those *voluntary Abortions*, and that horrid Practice of *Women murdering their Bastard Children*, alas! too frequent among us; sacrificing the *poor innocent Babes*, I doubt, more to avoid the Expence than the Shame, which would move Tears and Pity in the most Savage and inhuman Breast.

The number of Souls in *Ireland* being usually reckoned one Million and a half; of these I calculate there may be about
10 two hundred thousand Couple whose Wives are Breeders; from which number I substract thirty Thousand Couples, who are able to maintain their own Children; although I apprehend there cannot be so many, under *the present Distresses of the Kingdom*; but this being granted, there will remain an hundred and seventy thousand Breeders. I again Substract fifty Thousand, for those Women who miscarry, or whose Children die by accident, or disease within the Year. There only remain an hundred and twenty thousand Children of poor Parents annually born: The question there-
20 fore is, How this number shall be reared, and provided for? which, as I have already said, under the present Situation of Affairs, is utterly impossible by all the Methods hitherto proposed: For we can *neither employ them in Handicraft* or *Agriculture*; we neither build Houses, (I mean in the Country) nor cultivate Land: They can very seldom pick up a Livelyhood *by Stealing* until they arrive at six years Old; except where they are of towardly parts; although, I confess, they learn the Rudiments much earlier; during which time they can however be properly looked upon only
30 as *Probationers*; as I have been informed by a principal Gentleman in the County of Cavan, who protested to me, that he never knew above one or two Instances under the Age of six, even in a part of the Kingdom *so renowned for the quickest Proficiency in that Art*.

I am assured by our Merchants, that a Boy or a Girl

before twelve years Old, is no saleable Commodity; and even when they come to this Age, they will not yield above three Pounds, or three Pounds and half a Crown at most, on the Exchange; which cannot turn to Account either to the Parents or Kingdom, the Charge of Nutriment and Rags having been at least four times that Value.

I shall now therefore humbly propose my own Thoughts, which I hope will not be liable to the least Objection.

I have been assured by a very knowing *American* of my acquaintance in *London*, that a young healthy Child well 10 Nursed is, at a year Old, a most delicious nourishing and wholesome Food, whether *Stewed, Roasted, Baked*, or *Boiled*; and I make no doubt that it will equally serve in a *Fricasie*, or a *Ragoust*.

I do therefore humbly offer it to *publick consideration*, that of the Hundred and twenty thousand Children, already computed, twenty thousand may be reserved for Breed, whereof only one fourth part to be Males; which is more than we allow to *Sheep, black Cattle*, or *Swine*; and my Reason is, that these Children are seldom the Fruits of 20 Marriage, *a Circumstance not much regarded by our Savages*; therefore, *one Male* will be sufficient to serve *four Females*. That the remaining Hundred thousand may, at a year Old, be offered in Sale to the *Persons of Quality* and *Fortune*, through the Kingdom; always advising the Mother to let them suck plentifully in the last Month, so as to render them Plump, and Fat, for a good Table. A Child will make two Dishes at an Entertainment for Friends; and when the Family dines alone, the fore or hind Quarter will make a reasonable Dish; and seasoned with a little Pepper or Salt will 30 be very good Boiled on the fourth Day, especially in *Winter*.

I have reckoned upon a Medium, that a Child just born will weigh twelve pounds; and in a solar Year, if tolerably nursed, encreaseth to twenty eight Pounds.

I grant this Food will be somewhat dear, and therefore

very *proper for Landlords*; who, as they have already devoured most of the Parents seem to have the best Title to the Children. . . .

I think the Advantages by the Proposal which I have made are obvious and many, as well as of the highest Importance.

For *First*, as I have already observed, it would greatly lessen the *Number of Papists*, with whom we are yearly over-run; being the principal Breeders of the Nation, as
10 well as our most dangerous Enemies; and who stay at home on purpose with a Design *to deliver the Kingdom to the Pretender*; hoping to take their Advantage by the Absence of *so many good Protestants*, who have chosen rather to leave their Country, than stay at home, and pay Tithes against their Conscience, to an idolatrous *Episcopal Curate*.

Secondly, The poorer Tenants will have something valuable of their own, which by Law may be made lyable to Distress, and help to pay their Landlord's Rent; their Corn and Cattle being already seized, and *Money a Thing un-*
20 *known*.

Thirdly, Whereas the Maintenance of an hundred thousand Children, from two Years old, and upwards, cannot be computed at less than Ten Shillings a Piece *per Annum*, the Nation's Stock will be thereby increased fifty thousand Pounds *per Annum*; besides the Profit of a new Dish, introduced to the Tables of all *Gentlemen of Fortune* in the Kingdom, who have any Refinement in Taste; and the Money will circulate among our Selves, the Goods being entirely of our own Growth and Manufacture.

30 *Fourthly*, The constant Breeders, besides the Gain of eight Shillings *Sterling per Annum*, by the Sale of their Children, will be rid of the Charge of maintaining them after the first Year.

Fifthly, This Food would likewise bring great *Custom to Taverns*, where the Vintners will certainly be so prudent as to procure the best Receipts for dressing it to Perfection; and consequently have their Houses frequented by all the *fine Gentlemen,* who justly value themselves upon their Knowledge in good Eating; and a skilful Cook, who understands how to oblige his Guests, will contrive to make it as expensive as they please.

Sixthly, This would be a great Inducement to Marriage, which all wise Nations have either encouraged by Rewards, or enforced by Laws and Penalties. It would encrease the Care and Tenderness of Mothers towards their Children, 10 when they were sure of a Settlement for Life, to the poor Babes, provided in some Sort by the Publick, to their annual Profit instead of Expence. We should soon see an honest Emulation among the married Women, *which of them could bring the fattest Child to the Market.* Men would become as *fond* of their Wives, during the Time of their Pregnancy, as they are now of their *Mares* in Foal, their *Cows* in Calf, or *Sows* when they are ready to farrow; nor offer to beat or kick them (as is too *frequent* a Practice) for fear of a Miscarriage. 20

Many other Advantages might be enumerated. For Instance, the addition of some thousand Carcasses in our Exportation of Barreled Beef: The Propagation of *Swine's Flesh,* and Improvement in the Art of making good *Bacon,* so much wanted among us by the great Destruction of Pigs, too frequent at our Tables, which are no way comparable in Taste, or Magnificence to a well grown, fat yearling Child; which roasted whole will make a considerable Figure at a *Lord Mayor's Feast,* or any other Publick Entertainment. But this, and many others, I omit, being studious of 30 Brevity.

Supposing that one thousand Families in this City, would be constant Customers for Infant's Flesh; besides others who might have it at *merry Meetings,* particularly at *Weddings* and *Christenings*; I compute that *Dublin* would take off Annually about twenty thousand Carcasses; and the rest of the Kingdom (where probably they will be sold somewhat cheaper) the remaining eighty Thousand.

I can think of no one Objection, that will possibly be raised against this Proposal; unless it should be urged, that the Number of People will be thereby much lessened in the Kingdom. This I freely own, and it was indeed one principal Design in offering it to the World. I desire the Reader will observe, that I calculate my Remedy *for this one individual* 10 *Kingdom of* IRELAND, *and for no other that ever was, is, or, I think, ever can be upon Earth.* Therefore let no man talk to me of other Expedients: *Of taxing our Absentees at five Shillings a Pound: Of using neither Cloaths, nor Household Furniture, except what is of our own Growth and Manufacture: Of utterly rejecting the Materials and Instruments that promote Foreign Luxury: Of curing the Expensiveness of Pride, Vanity, Idleness, and Gaming in our Women: Of introducing a Vein of Parsimony, Prudence, and Temperance: Of learning to love our Country, wherein we differ even from* LAPLANDERS, *and* 20 *the Inhabitants of* TOPINAMBOO: *Of quitting our Animosities, and Factions, nor act any longer like the Jews, who were murdering one another at the very Moment their City was taken: Of being a little cautious not to sell our Country and Consciences for nothing: Of teaching Landlords to have at least one Degree of Mercy towards their Tenants.* Lastly, *Of putting a Spirit of Honesty, Industry, and Skill into our Shop-keepers; who, if a Resolution could now be taken to buy only our Native Goods, would immediately unite to cheat and exact upon us in the Price, the Measure, and the Goodness; nor could* 30 *ever yet be brought to make one fair Proposal of just Dealing, though often and earnestly invited to it.*

Therefore I repeat, let no Man talk to me of these and the like Expedients; till he hath at least some Glimpse of Hope, that there will ever be some hearty and sincere Attempt to put *them in Practice.*

But as to my self; having been wearied out for many Years with offering vain, idle, visionary Thoughts, and at length utterly despairing of Success, I fortunately fell upon this Proposal; which as it is wholly new, so it hath something *Solid* and *Real,* of no Expence and little Trouble, full in our own Power; and whereby we can incur no Danger in *disobliging* ENGLAND. For this kind of Commodity will not bear Exportation; the Flesh being of too tender a Consistence to admit a long Continuance in Salt; *although perhaps I could name a Country, which would be glad to eat up our whole* 10 *Nation without it.*

After all, I am not so violently bent upon my own Opinion, as to reject any Offer proposed by wise Men, which shall be found equally Innocent, Cheap, Easy, and Effectual. But before something of that Kind shall be advanced, in Contradiction to my Scheme, and offering a better; I desire the Author, or Authors, will be pleased maturely to consider two Points. *First,* As Things now stand, how they will be able to find Food and Raiment for a hundred Thousand useless Mouths and Backs. And *Secondly,* There being a round 20 Million of Creatures in Human Figure, throughout this Kingdom; whose whole Subsistence put into a common Stock, would leave them in Debt two Millions of Pounds *Sterling*; adding those, who are Beggars by Profession, to the Bulk of Farmers, Cottagers and Labourers, with their Wives and Children, who are Beggars in Effect; I desire those Politicians, who dislike my Overture, and may perhaps be so bold to attempt an Answer, that they will first ask the Parents of these Mortals, Whether they would not, at this Day, think it a great Happiness to have been sold for 30 Food at a Year Old, in the manner I prescribe; and thereby have avoided such a perpetual Scene of Misfortunes, as they have since gone through; by the *Oppression of Landlords*; the Impossibility of paying Rent without Money or Trade; the Want of common Sustenance, with neither House nor

Cloaths to cover them from the Inclemencies of the Weather; and the most inevitable Prospect of intailing the like, or greater Miseries, upon their Breed for ever.

I profess, in the Sincerity of my Heart, that I have not the least Personal Interest in endeavouring to promote this necessary Work; having no other Motive than the *Publick Good of my Country, by advancing our Trade, providing for Infants, relieving the Poor, and giving some Pleasure to the Rich.* I have no Children, by which I can propose to get a 10 single Penny; the youngest being nine Years old, and my Wife past Child-bearing.

From a poem *Occasioned by Sir William Temple's Late Illness and Recovery*

MALIGNANT goddess! bane to my repose, 81
Thou universal cause of all my woes;
Say, whence it comes that thou art grown of late
A poor amusement for my scorn and hate;
The malice thou inspir'st I never fail
On thee to wreak the tribute when I rail;
Fools common-place thou art, their weak ensconcing fort,
Th'appeal of dullness in the last resort:
Heaven with a parent's eye regarding earth,
Deals out to man the planet of his birth; 90
But sees thy meteor blaze about me shine,
And passing o'er, mistakes thee still for mine:
Ah, should I tell a secret yet unknown,
That thou ne'er hadst a being of thy own,
But a wild form dependent on the brain,
Scatt'ring loose features o'er the optic vein;
Troubling the chrystal fountain of the sight,
Which darts on poets eyes a trembling light;
Kindled while reason sleeps, but quickly flies,
Like antic shapes in dreams, from waking eyes: 100
In sum, a glitt'ring voice, a painted name,
A walking vapor, like thy sister fame. . . .
To thee I owe that fatal bent of mind, 131
Still to unhappy restless thoughts inclin'd;
To thee, what oft I vainly strive to hide,
That scorn of fools, by fools mistook for pride;
From thee whatever virtue takes its rise,
Grows a misfortune, or becomes a vice;
Such were thy rules to be poetically great,
'Stoop not to int'rest, flattery, or deceit;
'Nor with hir'd thoughts be thy devotion paid;
'Learn to disdain their mercenary aid; 140

Be this thy sure defence, thy brazen wall,
'Know no base action, at no guilt turn pale;
'And since unhappy distance thus denies
'T'expose thy soul, clad in this poor disguise;
'Since thy few ill-presented graces seem
'To breed contempt where thou hast hop'd esteem.'—
Madness like this no fancy ever seiz'd,
Still to be cheated, never to be pleas'd;
Since one false beam of joy in sickly minds
150 Is all the poor content delusion finds.—
There thy enchantment broke, and from this hour
I here renounce thy visionary pow'r;
And since thy essence on my breath depends,
Thus with a puff the whole delusion ends.

A Description of the Morning

Now hardly here and there an Hackney-Coach
Appearing, show'd the Ruddy Morns Approach.
Now *Betty* from her Masters Bed had flown,
And softly stole to discompose her own.
The Slipshod Prentice from his Masters Door,
Had par'd the Dirt, and Sprinkled round the Floor.
Now *Moll* had whirl'd her Mop with dext'rous Airs,
Prepar'd to Scrub the Entry and the Stairs.
The Youth with Broomy Stumps began to trace
10 The Kennel-Edge, where Wheels had worn the Place.
The Smallcoal-Man was heard with Cadence deep,
'Till drown'd in Shriller Notes of Chimney-Sweep,
Duns at his Lordships Gate began to meet,
And Brickdust *Moll* had Scream'd through half the Street.
The Turnkey now his Flock returning sees,
Duly let out a Nights to Steal for Fees.
The watchful Bailiffs take their silent Stands,
And School-Boys lag with Satchels in their Hands.

A City Shower

CAREFUL Observers may fortel the Hour
(By sure Prognosticks) when to dread a Show'r:
While Rain depends, the pensive Cat gives o'er
Her Frolicks, and pursues her Tail no more.
Returning Home at Night, you'll find the Sink
Strike your offended Sense with double Stink.
If you be wise, then go not far to Dine,
You'll spend in Coach-hire more than save in Wine.
A coming Show'r your shooting Corns presage,
Old Aches throb, your hollow Tooth will rage. 10
Sauntring in Coffee-house is *Dulman* seen;
He damns the Climate, and complains of Spleen.

MEAN while the South rising with dabbled Wings,
A Sable Cloud a-thwart the Welkin flings,
That swill'd more Liquor than it could contain,
And like a Drunkard gives it up again.
Brisk *Susan* whips her Linen from the Rope,
While the first drizzling Show'r is born aslope,
Such is that Sprinkling which some careless Quean
Flirts on you from her Mop, but not so clean. 20
You fly, invoke the Gods; then turning, stop
To rail; she singing, still whirls on her Mop.
Not yet, the Dust had shun'd th' unequal Strife,
But aided by the Wind, fought still for Life;
And wafted with its Foe by violent Gust,
'Twas doubtful which was Rain, and which was Dust.
Ah! where must needy Poet seek for Aid,
When Dust and Rain at once his Coat invade;
His only Coat, where Dust confus'd with Rain,
Roughen the Nap, and leave a mingled Stain. 30

NOW in contiguous Drops the Flood comes down,
Threat'ning with Deluge this *Devoted* Town.

To Shops in Crouds the dagged Females fly,
Pretend to cheapen Goods, but nothing buy.
The Templer spruce, while ev'ry Spout's a-broach,
Stays till 'tis fair, yet seems to call a Coach.
The tuck'd-up Sempstress walks with hasty Strides,
While Streams run down her oil'd Umbrella's Sides.
Here various Kinds by various Fortunes led,
40 Commence Acquaintance underneath a Shed.
Triumphant Tories, and desponding Whigs,
Forget their Fewds, and join to save their Wigs.
Box'd in a Chair the Beau impatient sits,
While Spouts run clatt'ring o'er the Roof by Fits;
And ever and anon with frightful Din
The Leather sounds, he trembles from within.
So when *Troy* Chair-men bore the Wooden Steed,
Pregnant with *Greeks*, impatient to be freed,
(Those Bully *Greeks*, who, as the Moderns do,
50 Instead of paying Chair-men, run them thro'.)
Laoco'n struck the Outside with his Spear,
And each imprison'd Hero quak'd for Fear.

Now from all Parts the swelling Kennels flow,
And bear their Trophies with them as they go:
Filth of all Hues and Odours seem to tell
What Street they sail'd from, by their sight and Smell.
They, as each Torrent drives, with rapid Force
From *Smithfield*, or St. *Pulchre*'s shape their Course,
And in huge Confluent join at *Snow-Hill* Ridge,
60 Fall from the *Conduit* prone to *Holborn-Bridge*.
Sweepings from Butchers Stalls, Dung, Guts, and Blood,
Drown'd Puppies, stinking Sprats, all drench'd in Mud,
Dead Cats and Turnip-Tops come tumbling down the Flood.

97

A Satirical Elegy

His Grace! impossible! what dead!
Of old age too, and in his bed!
And could that Mighty Warrior fall?
And so inglorious, after all!
Well, since he's gone, no matter how,
The last loud trump must wake him now:
And, trust me, as the noise grows stronger,
He'd wish to sleep a little longer.
And could he be indeed so old
As by the news-papers we're told? 10
Threescore, I think, is pretty high;
'Twas time in conscience he should die.
This world he cumber'd long enough;
He burnt his candle to the snuff;
And that's the reason, some folks think,
He left behind *so great a s - - - k.*
Behold his funeral appears,
Nor widow's sighs, nor orphan's tears,
Wont at such times each heart to pierce,
Attend the progress of his herse. 20
But what of that, his friends may say,
He had those honours in his day.
True to his profit and his pride,
He made them weep before he dy'd.

Come hither, all ye empty things,
Ye bubbles rais'd by breath of Kings;
Who float upon the tide of state,
Come hither, and behold your fate.
Let pride be taught by this rebuke,
How very mean a thing's a Duke; 30
From all his ill-got honours flung,
Turn'd to that dirt from whence he sprung.

Hor. Lib. 2. Sat. 6

I OFTEN wish'd, that I had clear
For Life, six hundred Pounds a Year,
A handsome House to lodge a Friend,
A River at my Garden's End,
A Terras Walk, and half a Rood
Of Land set out to plant a Wood.

Well, now I have all this and more,
I ask not to increase my Store,
[But here a Grievance seems to lie,
10 All this is mine but till I die;
I can't but think 'twould sound more clever,
To me and to my Heirs for ever.

If I ne'er got, or lost a groat,
By any *Trick*, or any *Fault*;
And if I pray by Reason's rules,
And not like forty other Fools:
As thus, 'Vouchsafe, Oh gracious Maker!
'To grant me this and t'other Acre:
'Or if it be thy Will and Pleasure
20 'Direct my Plow to find a Treasure:'
But only what my Station fits,
And to be kept in my right wits.
Preserve, Almighty Providence!
Just what you gave me, Competence:
And let me in these Shades compose
Something in Verse as true as Prose;
Remov'd from all th' ambitious Scene,
Nor puff'd by Pride, nor sunk by Spleen.]
But should be perfectly content,
30 Could I but live on this side *Trent*;
Nor cross the *Channel* twice a Year,
To spend six Months with *Statesmen* here.

I must by all means come to Town,
'Tis for the Service of the Crown.
'*Lewis*; the *Dean* will be of Use,
'Send for him up, take no Excuse.
The Toil, the Danger of the Seas;
Great Ministers ne'er think of these;
Or let it cost Five hundred Pound,
No matter where the Money's found; 40
It is but so much more in Debt,
And that they ne'er consider'd yet.

'Good Mr. *Dean* go change your Gown,
'Let my Lord know you're come to Town.
I hurry me in haste away,
Not thinking it is Levee-Day;
And find his Honour in a Pound,
Hemm'd by a triple Circle round,
Chequer'd with Ribbons blew and green;
How should I thrust my self between? 50
Some Wag observes me thus perplext,
And smiling, whispers to the next,
'I thought the *D - - - n* had been too proud,
'To justle here among a Crowd.
Another in a surly Fit,
Tells me I have more Zeal than Wit,
'So eager to express your Love,
'You ne'er consider whom you shove,
'But rudely press before a Duke.
I own, I'm pleas'd with this Rebuke, 60
And take it kindly meant to show
What I desire the World should know.

I get a Whisper, and withdraw,
When twenty Fools I never saw
Come with Petitions fairly pen'd,
Desiring I would stand their Friend.

This, humbly offers me his Case - - -
That, begs my Interest for a Place - - -
A hundred other Men's Affairs
70 Like Bees, are humming in my Ears.
'To morrow my Appeal comes on,
'Without your Help the Cause is gone - -
The Duke expects my Lord and you,
About some great Affair, at Two - - -
'Put my Lord *Bolingbroke* in Mind,
'To get my Warrant quickly signed:
'Consider, 'tis my first Request. - - -
Be satisfy'd, I'll do my best: - - -
Then presently he falls to teize,
80 'You may for certain, if you please;
'I doubt not, if his Lordship knew - - -
'And Mr. *Dean*, one Word from you - - -

'Tis (let me see) three Years and more,
(*October* next, it will be four)
Since HARLEY bid me first attend,
And chose me for an humble Friend;
Would take me in his Coach to chat,
And question me of this and that;
As, 'What's a-Clock?' And, 'How's the Wind?
90 'Whose Chariot's that we left behind?
Or gravely try to read the Lines
Writ underneath the Country *Signs*;
Or, 'Have you nothing new to day
'From *Pope*, from *Parnel*, or from *Gay?*
Such Tattle often entertains
My Lord and me as far as *Stains*,
As once a week we travel down
To *Windsor*, and again to Town,
Where all that passes, *inter nos*,
100 Might be proclaim'd at *Charing-Cross*.

Yet some I know with Envy swell,
Because they see me us'd so well:
'How think you of our Friend the *Dean?*
'I wonder what some People mean;
'My Lord and he are grown so great,
'Always together, *tête à tête:*
'What, they admire him for his Jokes - - -
'See but the Fortune of some Folks!
There flies about a strange Report
Of some Express arriv'd at Court; 110
I'm stopt by all the Fools I meet,
And catechis'd in ev'ry Street.
'You, Mr. *Dean* frequent the Great;
'Inform us, will the Emp'ror treat?
'Or do the Prints and Papers lye?
Faith Sir, you know as much as I.
'Ah Doctor, how you love to jest?
''Tis now no Secret - - I protest
'Tis one to me. - - 'Then, tell us, pray
'When are the Troops to have their Pay? 120
And, though I solemnly declare
I know no more than my *Lord Mayor,*
They stand amaz'd, and think me grown
The closest Mortal ever known.

Thus in a Sea of Folly tost,
My choicest Hours of Life are lost:
Yet always wishing to retreat;
Oh, could I see my Country Seat.
There leaning near a gentle Brook,
Sleep, or peruse some antient Book; 130
And there in sweet Oblivion drown
Those Cares that haunt the Court and Town.

On Stella's Birthday, 1718–19

STELLA this Day is thirty four,
(We won't dispute a Year or more)
However Stella, be not troubled,
Although thy Size and Years are doubled,
Since first I saw Thee at Sixteen
The brightest Virgin of the Green,
So little is thy Form declin'd
Made up so largly in thy Mind.
Oh, would it please the Gods to split
10 Thy beauty, Size, and Years, and Wit,
No Age could furnish out a Pair
Of Nymphs so gracefull, Wise and fair
With half the Lustre of Your Eyes,
With half thy Wit, thy Years and Size:
And then before it grew too late,
How should I beg of gentle Fate,
(That either Nymph might have her Swain,)
To split my Worship too in twain.

On Stella's Birthday, 1726–7

THIS Day, whate'er the Fates decree,
Shall still be kept with Joy by me:
This Day then, let us not be told,
That you are sick, and I grown old,
Nor think on our approaching Ills,
And talk of Spectacles and Pills;
To morrow will be Time enough
To hear such mortifying Stuff.
Yet, since from Reason may be brought
10 A better and more pleasing Thought,
Which can in spite of all Decays,
Support a few remaining Days:
From not the gravest of Divines,
Accept for once some serious Lines.

Although we now can form no more
Long Schemes of Life, as heretofore;
Yet you, while Time is running fast,
Can look with Joy on what is past.

Were future Happiness and Pain,
A mere Contrivance of the Brain, 20
As Atheists argue, to entice,
And fit their Proselytes for Vice;
(The only Comfort they propose,
To have Companions in their Woes.)
Grant this the Case, yet sure 'tis hard,
That Virtue, stil'd its own Reward,
And by all Sages understood
To be the chief of human Good,
Should acting, die, nor leave behind
Some lasting Pleasure in the Mind, 30
Which by Remembrance will assuage,
Grief, Sickness, Poverty, and Age;
And strongly shoot a radiant Dart,
To shine through Life's declining Part.

Say, *Stella,* feel you no Content,
Reflecting on a Life well spent?
Your skilful Hand employ'd to save
Despairing Wretches from the Grave;
And then supporting with your Store,
Those whom you dragg'd from Death before: 40
(So Providence on Mortals waits,
Preserving what it first creates)
Your gen'rous Boldness to defend
An innocent and absent Friend;
That Courage which can make you just,
To Merit humbled in the Dust:
The Detestation you express
For Vice in all its glitt'ring Dress:

That Patience under tort'ring Pain,
50 Where stubborn Stoicks would complain.

Must these like empty Shadows pass,
Or Forms reflected from a Glass?
Or mere Chimæra's in the Mind,
That fly and leave no Marks behind?
Does not the Body thrive and grow
By Food of twenty Years ago?
And, had it not been still supply'd,
It must a thousand Times have dy'd.
Then, who with Reason can maintain,
60 That no Effects of Food remain?
And, is not Virtue in Mankind
The Nutriment that feeds the Mind?
Upheld by each good Action past,
And still continued by the last:
Then, who with Reason can pretend,
That all Effects of Virtue end?

Believe me *Stella*, when you show
That true Contempt for Things below,
Nor prize your Life for other Ends
70 Than merely to oblige your Friends;
Your former Actions claim their Part,
And join to fortify your Heart.
For Virtue in her daily Race,
Like *Janus*, bears a double Face;
Looks back with Joy where she has gone,
And therefore goes with Courage on.
She at your sickly Couch will wait,
And guide you to a better State.

O then, whatever Heav'n intends,
80 Take Pity on your pitying Friends;

Nor let your Ills affect your Mind,
To fancy they can be unkind.
Me, surely me, you ought to spare,
Who gladly would your Suff'rings share;
Or give my Scrap of Life to you,
And think it far beneath your Due;
You, to whose Care so oft I owe,
That I'm alive to tell you so.

From *The Journal of a Modern Lady*

Now Voices over Voices rise; 174
While each to be the loudest vies,
They contradict, affirm, dispute,
No single Tongue one Moment mute;
All mad to speak, and none to hearken,
They set the very Lap-Dog barking;
Their Chattering makes a louder Din 180
Than Fish-Wives o'er a Cup of Gin:
Not School-boys at a Barring-out,
Rais'd ever such incessant Rout:
The Jumbling Particles of Matter
In Chaos made not such a Clatter:
Far less the Rabble roar and rail,
When drunk with sour Election Ale.

Nor do they trust their Tongue alone,
To speak a Language of their own;
But read a Nod, a Shrug, a Look, 190
Far better than a printed Book;
Convey a Libel in a Frown,
And wink a Reputation down;
Or by the tossing of the Fan,
Describe the Lady and the Man.

Verses on the Death of Dr. Swift

As *Rochefoucault* his Maxims drew
From Nature, I believe 'em true:
They argue no corrupted Mind
In him; the Fault is in Mankind.

This Maxim more than all the rest
Is thought too base for human Breast;
'In all Distresses of our Friends
'We first consult our private Ends,
'While Nature kindly bent to ease us,
10 'Points out some Circumstance to please us. . . .

What Poet would not grieve to see,
His Brethren write as well as he?
But rather than they should excel,
He'd wish his Rivals all in Hell. . . .

47 In Pope, I cannot read a Line,
But with a Sigh, I wish it mine:
When he can in one Couplet fix
50 More Sense than I can do in Six:
It gives me such a jealous Fit,
I cry, Pox take him, and his Wit.

Why must I be outdone by Gay,
In my own hum'rous biting Way?

Arbuthnot is no more my Friend,
Who dares to Irony pretend;
Which I was born to introduce,
Refin'd it first, and shew'd its Use.

St. John, as well as Pultney knows,
60 That I had some repute for Prose;
And till they drove me out of Date,
Could maul a Minister of State:

If they have mortify'd my Pride,
And made me throw my Pen aside;
If with such Talents Heav'n hath blest 'em
Have I not Reason to detest 'em?

To all my Foes, dear Fortune, send
Thy Gifts, but never to my Friend:
I tamely can endure the first,
But, this with Envy makes me burst. 70

* * *

'BEHOLD the fatal Day arrive! 147
'How is the Dean? He's just alive.
'Now the departing Prayer is read:
'He hardly breathes. The Dean is dead. 150
'Before the Passing-Bell begun,
'The News thro' half the Town has run.
'O, may we all for Death prepare!
'What has he left? And who's his Heir?
'I know no more than what the News is,
''Tis all bequeath'd to publick Uses.
'To publick Use! A perfect Whim!
'What had the Publick done for him!
'Meer Envy, Avarice, and Pride!
'He gave it all:—But first he dy'd. 160
'And had the Dean, in all the Nation,
'No worthy Friend, no poor Relation?
'So ready to do Strangers good,
'Forgetting his own Flesh and Blood?

Now Grub-Street Wits are all employ'd;
With Elegies, the Town is cloy'd:
Some Paragraph in ev'ry Paper,
[1]To *curse* the *Dean*, or *bless* the *Drapier*.

[1] *The Author imagines, that the Scriblers of the prevailing Party, which he always opposed, will libel him after his Death; but that others will remember him with Gratitude, who consider the Service he had done to* Ireland, *under the Name of* M. B. *Drapier, by utterly defeating the*

THE Doctors tender of their Fame,
170 Wisely on me lay all the Blame:
'We must confess his Case was nice;
'But he would never take Advice:
'Had he been rul'd, for ought appears,
'He might have liv'd these Twenty Years:
'For when we open'd him we found,
'That all his vital Parts were sound.

FROM *Dublin* soon to *London* spread,
[1]'Tis told at Court, the Dean is dead.

[2]KIND Lady *Suffolk* in the Spleen,
180 Runs laughing up to tell the Queen.
The Queen, so Gracious, Mild, and Good,
Cries, 'Is he gone? 'Tis time he shou'd.
'He's dead you say; why let him rot;
[3]'I'm glad the Medals were forgot.

destructive Project of Wood'*s Half-pence, in five Letters to the People of* Ireland, *at that Time read universally, and convincing every Reader.*

[1] *The Dean supposeth himself to dye in* Ireland.

[2] *Mrs.* Howard, *afterwards Countess of* Suffolk, *then of the Bed-chamber to the Queen, professed much Friendship for the Dean. The Queen then Princess, sent a dozen times to the Dean* (*then in* London) *with her Command to attend her; which at last he did, by Advice of all his Friends. She often sent for him afterwards, and always treated him very Graciously. He taxed her with a Present worth Ten Pounds, which she promised before he should return to* Ireland, *but on his taking Leave, the Medals were not ready.*

[3] *The Medals were to be sent to the Dean in four Months, but she forgot them, or thought them too dear. The Dean, being in* Ireland, *sent Mrs.* Howard *a Piece of* Indian *Plad made in that Kingdom: which the Queen seeing took from her, and wore it herself, and sent to the Dean for as much as would cloath herself and Children, desiring he would send the Charge of it. He did the former. It cost thirty-five Pounds, but he said he would have nothing except the Medals. He was the Summer following in* England, *was treated as usual, and she being then Queen, the Dean was promised a Settlement in* England, *but returned as he went, and, instead of Favour or Medals, hath been ever since under her Majesty's Displeasure.*

'I promis'd them, I own; but when?
'I only was the Princess then;
'But now as Consort of the King,
'You know 'tis quite a different Thing.

* * *

SUPPOSE me dead; and then suppose
A Club assembled at the *Rose*; 300
Where from Discourse of this and that,
I grow the Subject of their Chat:
And, while they toss my Name about,
With Favour some, and some without;
One quite indiff'rent in the Cause,
My Character impartial draws:

'THE Dean, if we believe Report,
'Was never ill receiv'd at Court:
'As for his Works in Verse and Prose,
'I own my self no Judge of those: 310
'Nor, can I tell what Criticks thought 'em;
'But, this I know, all People bought 'em;
'As with a moral View design'd
'To cure the Vices of Mankind:
'His Vein, ironically grave,
'Expos'd the Fool, and lash'd the Knave:
'To steal a Hint was never known,
'But what he writ was all his own.

'HE never thought an Honour done him,
'Because a Duke was proud to own him: 320
'Would rather slip aside, and chuse
'To talk with Wits in dirty Shoes:
'Despis'd the Fools with Stars and Garters,
'So often seen caressing *Chartres:*
'He never courted Men in Station,
'*Nor Persons had in Admiration*;

'Of no Man's Greatness was afraid,
'Because he sought for no Man's Aid.
'Though trusted long in great Affairs,
330 'He gave himself no haughty Airs:
'Without regarding private Ends,
'Spent all his Credit for his Friends:
'And only chose the Wise and Good;
'No Flatt'rers; no Allies in Blood;
'But succour'd Virtue in Distress,
'And seldom fail'd of good Success;
'As Numbers in their Hearts must own,
'Who, but for him, had been unknown.

'WITH Princes kept a due Decorum,
340 'But never stood in Awe before 'em:
'He follow'd *David*'s Lesson just,
'*In Princes never put thy Trust.*
'And, would you make him truly sower;
'Provoke him with *a slave in Power:*
'The *Irish* Senate, if you nam'd,
'With what Impatience he declaim'd!
'Fair LIBERTY was all his Cry;
'For her he stood prepar'd to die;
'For her he boldly stood alone;
350 'For her he oft expos'd his own.
[1]'Two Kingdoms, just as Faction led,
'Had set a Price upon his Head;

1 *In the Year* 1713, *the late Queen was prevailed with by an Address of the House of Lords in* England, *to publish a Proclamation, promising Three Hundred Pounds to whatever Person would discover the Author of a Pamphlet called,* The Publick Spirit of the Whiggs; *and in* Ireland, *in the year* 1724, *my Lord* Carteret *at his first coming into the Government, was prevailed on to issue a Proclamation for promising the like Reward of Three Hundred Pounds, to any Person who could discover the Author of a Pamphlet called,* The Drapier's Fourth Letter, *&c. writ against that destructive Project of coining Half-pence for* Ireland; *but in neither Kingdoms was the Dean discovered.*

'But, not a Traytor cou'd be found,
'To sell him for Six Hundred Pound.

'HAD he but spar'd his Tongue and Pen,
'He might have rose like other Men:
'But, Power was never in his Thought;
'And, Wealth he valu'd not a Groat:
'Ingratitude he often found,
'And pity'd those who meant the Wound: 360
'But, kept the Tenor of his Mind,
'To merit well of human Kind:
'Nor made a Sacrifice of those
'Who still were true, to please his Foes.
[1]'He labour'd many a fruitless Hour
'To reconcile his Friends in Power;
'Saw Mischief by a Faction brewing,
'While they pursu'd each others Ruin.
'But, finding vain was all his Care,
'He left the Court in meer Despair. 370

'AND, oh! how short are human Schemes!
'Here ended all our golden Dreams.
'What ST. JOHN's Skill in State Affairs,
'What ORMOND's *Valour*, OXFORD's Cares,
'To save their sinking Country lent,
'Was all destroy'd by one Event.
[2]'Too soon that precious Life was ended,
'On which alone, our Weal depended.

[1] *Queen* ANNE'*s Ministry fell to Variance from the first Year after their Ministry began:* Harcourt *the Chancellor,* and *Lord* Bolingbroke *the Secretary, were discontented with the Treasurer* Oxford, *for his too much Mildness to the Whig Party; this Quarrel grew higher every Day till the Queen's Death: The Dean, who was the only Person that endeavoured to reconcile them, found it impossible; and thereupon retired to the Country about ten Weeks before that fatal Event: Upon which he returned to his Deanry in* Dublin, *where for many Years he was worryed by the new People in Power, and had Hundreds of Libels writ against him in* England.

[2] *In the Height of the Quarrel between the Ministers, the Queen died.*

[1]'When up a dangerous Faction starts,
380 'With Wrath and Vengeance in their Hearts:
'*By solemn League and Cov'nant bound,*
'To ruin, slaughter, and confound;
'To turn Religion to a Fable,
'And make the Government a *Babel:*
'Pervert the Law, disgrace the Gown,
'Corrupt the Senate, rob the Crown;
'To sacrifice old *England*'s Glory,
'And make her infamous in Story.
'When such a Tempest shook the Land,
390 'How could unguarded Virtue stand?

'WITH Horror, Grief, Despair the Dean
'Beheld the dire destructive Scene:
'His Friends in Exile, or the Tower,
[2]'Himself within the Frown of Power;
'Pursu'd by base envenom'd Pens,
[3]'Far to the Land of Slaves and Fens;
'A servile Race in Folly nurs'd,
'Who truckle most, when treated worst.

'BY Innocence and Resolution,
400 'He bore continual Persecution;

[1] *Upon Queen* ANNE'*s Death the Whig Faction was restored to Power, which they exercised with the utmost Rage and Revenge; impeached and banished the Chief Leaders of the Church Party, and stripped all their Adherents of what Employments they had, after which* England *was never known to make so mean a Figure in* Europe. *The greatest Preferments in the Church in both Kingdoms were given to the most ignorant Men, Fanaticks were publickly caressed,* Ireland *utterly ruined and enslaved, only great Ministers heaping up Millions, and so Affairs continue until this present third Day of May,* 1732, *and are likely to go on in the same Manner.*

[2] *Upon the Queen's Death, the Dean returned to live in* Dublin, *at his Deanry-House: Numberless Libels were writ against him in* England, *as a Jacobite; he was insulted in the Street, and at Nights was forced to be attended by his Servants armed.*

[3] *The Land of Slaves and Fens, is* Ireland.

'While Numbers to Preferment rose;
'Whose Merits were, to be his Foes.
'When, *ev'n his own familiar Friends*
'Intent upon their private Ends;
'Like Renegadoes now he feels,
'*Against him lifting up their Heels.*

'The Dean did by his Pen defeat
[1]'An infamous destructive Cheat.
'Taught Fools their Int'rest how to know;
'And gave them Arms to ward the Blow. 410
'Envy hath own'd it was his doing,
'To save that helpless Land from Ruin,
'While they who at the Steerage stood,
'And reapt the Profit, sought his Blood.

'To save them from their evil Fate,
'In him was held a Crime of State.
[2]'A wicked Monster on the Bench,
'Whose Fury Blood could never quench;
'As vile and profligate a Villain,
'As modern [3]*Scroggs*, or old *Tressilian*; 420

[1] *One* Wood, *a Hardware-man from* England, *had a Patent for coining Copper Half-pence in* Ireland, *to the Sum of* 108,000 l. *which in the Consequence, must leave that Kingdom without Gold or Silver* (*See* Drapier's *Letters*.)

[2] *One* Whitshed *was then Chief Justice: He had some Years before prosecuted a Printer for a Pamphlet writ by the Dean, to perswade the People of* Ireland *to wear their own Manufactures.* Whitshed *sent the Jury down eleven Times, and kept them nine Hours, until they were forced to bring in a special Verdict. He sat as Judge afterwards on the Tryal of the Printer of the* Drapier'*s Fourth Letter; but the Jury, against all he could say or swear, threw out the Bill: All the Kingdom took the* Drapier'*s Part, except the Courtiers, or those who expected Places. The* Drapier *was celebrated in many Poems and Pamphlets: His Sign was set up in most Streets of* Dublin (*where many of them still continue*) *and in several Country Towns.*

[3] Scroggs *was Chief Justice under King* Charles *the Second: His Judgment always varied in State Tryals, according to Directions from Court.* Tressilian *was a wicked Judge, hanged above three hundred Years ago.*

'Who long all Justice had discarded,
'Nor fear'd he GOD, nor Man regarded;
'Vow'd on the Dean his Rage to vent,
'And make him of his Zeal repent;
'But Heav'n his Innocence defends,
'The grateful People stand his Friends:
'Not Strains of Law, nor Judges Frown,
'Nor Topicks brought to please the Crown,
'Nor Witness hir'd, nor Jury pick'd,
430 'Prevail to bring him in convict.

[1]'IN Exile with a steady Heart,
'He spent his Life's declining Part;
'Where, Folly, Pride, and Faction sway,
[2]'Remote from ST. JOHN, POPE, and GAY.

[3]'HIS Friendship there to few confin'd,
'Were always of the midling Kind:
'No Fools of Rank, a mungril Breed,
'Who fain would pass for Lords indeed:
[4]'Where Titles give no Right or Power,
440 'And Peerage is a wither'd Flower,
'He would have held it a Disgrace,
'If such a Wretch had known his Face.
'On Rural Squires, that Kingdom's Bane,
'He vented oft his Wrath in vain:

[1] *In* Ireland, *which he had Reason to call a Place of Exile; to which Country nothing could have driven him, but the Queen's Death, who had determined to fix him in* England, *in Spight of the Dutchess of* Somerset, *&c.*

[2] Henry St. John, *Lord Viscount* Bolingbroke, *mentioned before.*

[3] *In* Ireland *the Dean was not acquainted with one single Lord Spiritual or Temporal. He only conversed with private Gentlemen of the Clergy or Laity, and but a small Number of either.*

[4] *The Peers of* Ireland *lost a great Part of their Jurisdiction by one single Act, and tamely submitted to this infamous Mark of Slavery without the least Resentment, or Remonstrance.*

[1]'Biennial Squires, to Market brought;
'Who sell their Souls and Votes for Naught;
'The Nation stript go joyful back,
'To rob the Church, their Tenants rack,
'Go Snacks with Thieves and [2]Rapparees,
'And, keep the Peace, to pick up Fees: 450
'In every Jobb to have a Share,
'A Jayl or [3]Barrack to repair;
'And turn the Tax for publick Roads
'Commodious to their own Abodes.

'PERHAPS I may allow, the Dean
'Had too much Satyr in his Vein;
'And seem'd determin'd not to starve it,
'Because no Age could more deserve it.
'Yet, Malice never was his Aim;
'He lash'd the Vice but spar'd the Name. 460
'No Individual could resent,
'Where Thousands equally were meant.
'His Satyr points at no Defect,
'But what all Mortals may correct;
'For he abhorr'd that senseless Tribe,
'Who call it Humour when they jibe:
'He spar'd a Hump or crooked Nose,
'Whose Owners set not up for Beaux.
'True genuine Dulness mov'd his Pity,
'Unless it offer'd to be witty. 470

1 *The Parliament (as they call it) in* Ireland *meet but once in two Years; and, after giving five Times more than they can afford, return Home to reimburse themselves by all Country Jobs and Oppressions, of which some few only are here mentioned.*

2 *The Highway-Men in* Ireland *are, since the late Wars there, usually called Rapparees, which was a Name given to those* Irish *Soldiers who in small Parties used, at that Time, to plunder the Protestants.*

3 *The Army in* Ireland *is lodged in Barracks, the building and repairing whereof, and other Charges, have cost a prodigious Sum to that unhappy Kingdom.*

'Those, who their Ignorance confess'd,
'He ne'er offended with a Jest;
'But laugh'd to hear an Idiot quote,
'A Verse from *Horace*, learn'd by Rote.

'HE knew an hundred pleasant Stories,
'With all the Turns of *Whigs* and *Tories:*
'Was chearful to his dying Day,
'And Friends would let him have his Way.

'HE gave the little Wealth he had,
480 'To build a House for Fools and Mad:
'And shew'd by one satyric Touch,
'No Nation wanted it so much:
[1]'That Kingdom he hath left his Debtor,
'I wish it soon may have a Better.

The Day of Judgement

WITH a Whirl of Thought oppress'd,
I sink from Reverie to Rest.
An horrid Vision seiz'd my Head,
I saw the Graves give up their Dead.
Jove, arm'd with Terrors, burst the Skies,
And Thunder roars, and Light'ning flies!
Amaz'd, confus'd, its Fate unknown,
The World stands Trembling at his Throne.
While each pale Sinner hangs his Head,
10 Jove, nodding, shook the Heav'ns, and said,
'Offending Race of Human Kind,
By Nature, Reason, Learning, blind;
You who thro' Frailty step'd aside,
And you who never fell—*thro' Pride*;
You who in different Sects have shamm'd,
And come to see each other damn'd;

[1] *Meaning* Ireland, *where he now lives, and probably may dye.*

(So some Folks told you, but they knew
No more of Jove's Designs than you)
The World's mad Business now is o'er,
And I resent these Pranks no more. 20
I to such Blockheads set my Wit!
I damn such Fools!—Go, go, you're bit.'

JOURNAL TO STELLA

Letter V

[Saturday] London, Sept. 30, 1710.

HAN'T I brought myself into a fine *premunire* to begin writing letters in whole sheets, and now I dare not leave it off. I can't tell whether you like these journal letters: I believe they would be dull to me to read them over; but, perhaps, little MD is pleased to know how Presto passes his time in her absence. I always begin my last the same day I ended my former. I told you where I dined to-day at a tavern with Stratford: Lewis, who is a great favourite of Harley's, was to have been with us; but he was hurried to Hampton-court, and sent his excuse; and that next Wednesday he would introduce me to Harley. 'Tis good to see what a lamentable confession the Whigs all make me of my ill usage: but I mind them not. I am already represented to Harley as a discontented person, that was used ill for not being Whig enough; and I hope for good usage from him. The Tories dryly tell me, I may make my fortune, if I please; but I do not understand them, or rather, I do understand them.

Oct. 1. To-day I dined at Molesworth's, the Florence envoy: and sat this evening with my friend Darteneuf, whom you have heard me talk of; the greatest punner of this town next myself. Have you smoakt the *Tatler* that I writ? It is much liked here, and I think it is a pure one. To-morrow I go with Delaval the Portugal envoy, to dine with Lord Halifax near Hampton-court. Your Manley's brother, a parliament-man here, has gotten an employment; and I am informed uses much interest to preserve his brother: and, to-day, I spoke to the elder Frankland to engage his father, (post-master here) and I hope he will be safe, although he is cruelly hated by all the Tories of Ireland.

I have almost finished my lampoon, and will print it for revenge on a certain great person. It has cost me but three shillings in meat and drink since I came here, as thin as the town is. I laugh to see myself so disengaged in these revolutions. Well, I must leave off and go write to sir John Stanley, to desire him to engage lady Hyde as my mistress to engage lord Hyde in favour of Mr. Pratt.

2. Lord Halifax was at Hampton-court at his lodgings, and I dined with him there with Methuen, and Delaval, and the late attorney-general. I went to the drawing-room before dinner, (for the queen was at Hampton-court) and expected to see *nobody*; but I met acquaintance enough. I walked in the gardens, saw the cartons of Raphael, and other things, and with great difficulty got from lord Halifax, who would have kept me to-morrow to shew me his house and park, and improvements. We left Hampton-court at sun-set, and got here in a chariot and two horses time enough by star-light. That's something charms me mightily about London; that you go dine a dozen miles off in October, stay all day, and return so quickly: you cannot do any thing like this in Dublin. I writ a second penny-post letter to your mother, and hear nothing of her. Did I tell you that earl Berkeley died last Sunday was se'n-night, at Berkeley-castle, of a dropsy? Lord Halifax began a health to me to-day: it was the Resurrection of the Whigs, which I refused unless he would add their Reformation too: and I told him he was the only Whig in England I loved, or had any good opinion of. . . .

7. I wonder when this letter will be finished: it must go by Tuesday, that's certain; and if I have one from MD before, I will not answer it, that's as certain too! 'Tis now morning, and I did not finish my papers for Mr. Harley last night; for you must understand Presto was sleepy, and made blunders and blots. Very pretty that I must be writing to young women in a morning fresh and fasting, faith. Well,

good morrow to you; and so I go to business, and lay aside
this paper till night, sirrahs.—At night. Jack How told
Harley, that if there were a lower place in Hell than another,
it was reserved for his porter, who tells lies so gravely, and
with so civil a manner. This porter I have had to deal with,
going this evening at four to visit Mr. Harley, by his own
appointment. But the fellow told me no lie, though I suspected every word he said. He told me his master was just
gone to dinner, with much company, and desired I would
10 come an hour hence, which I did, expecting to hear Mr.
Harley was gone out; but they had just done dinner. Mr.
Harley came out to me, brought me in, and presented me to
his son-in-law, lord Doblane (or some such name) and his
own son, and, among others, Will Penn the quaker: we sat
two hours drinking as good wine as you do; and two hours
more he and I alone; where he heard me tell my business;
entered into it with all kindness; askt for my powers, and
read them; and read likewise a memorial I had drawn up,
and put it in his pocket to show the queen; told me the
20 measures he would take; and, in short, said every thing I
could wish: told me he must bring Mr. St. John (secretary
of state) and me acquainted; and spoke so many things of
personal kindness and esteem for me, that I am inclined half
to believe what some friends have told me, That he would
do every thing to bring me over. He has desired to dine with
me (what a comical mistake was that) I mean he has desired
me to dine with him on Tuesday, and after four hours being
with him, set me down at St. James's Coffee-house, in a
hackney-coach. All this is odd and comical, if you consider
30 him and me. He knew my Christian name very well. I could
not forbear saying thus much upon this matter, although
you will think it tedious. But I'll tell you; you must know,
'tis fatal to me to be a scoundrel and a prince the same day:
for being to see him at four, I could not engage myself to
dine at any friend's; so I went to Tooke, to give him a ballad

and dine with him; but he was not at home: so I was forced to go to a blind chop-house, and dine for ten-pence upon gill-ale, bad broth, and three chops of mutton; and then go reeking from thence to the first minister of state. And now I am going in charity to send Steele a *Tatler*, who is very low of late. I think I am civiller than I used to be; and have not used the expression of (*you in* Ireland) and (*we in* England), as I did when I was here before, to your great indignation. —— They may talk of the *you know what*; but, gad, if it had not been for that, I should never have been able to get 10 the access I have had; and if that helps me to succeed, then that *same thing* will be serviceable to the church. But how far we must depend upon new friends, I have learnt by long practice, though I think among great ministers, they are just as good as old ones. And so I think this important day has made a great hole in this side of the paper; and the fiddle faddles of to-morrow and Monday will make up the rest; and, besides, I shall see Harley on Tuesday before this letter goes.

8. I must tell you a great piece of refinement of Harley. 20 He charged me to come to him often: I told him I was loth to trouble him in so much business as he had, and desired I might have leave to come at his levee; which he immediately refused, and said, That was not a place for friends to come to. 'Tis now but morning, and I have got a foolish trick, I must say something to MD when I wake, and wish them a good morrow; for this is not a shaving-day, Sunday, so I have time enough: but get you gone, you rogues, I must go write: yes, 'twill vex me to the blood if any of these long letters should miscarry: if they do, I will shrink to half 30 sheets again; but then what will you do to make up the journal? there will be ten days of Presto's life lost; and that will be a sad thing, faith and troth.—At night. I was at a loss to-day for a dinner, unless I would have gone a great way, so I dined with some friends that board hereabout, as

a spunger, and this evening sir Andrew Fountain would needs have me go to the tavern, where, for two bottles of wine, Portugal and Florence, among three of us, we had sixteen shillings to pay; but if ever he catches me so again, I'll spend as many pounds: and therefore I have it among my extraordinaries: but we had a neck of mutton dressed *à la Maintenon*, that the dog could not eat: and it is now twelve o'clock, and I must go sleep. I hope this letter will go before I have MD's third. Do you believe me? and yet, faith,
10 I long for MD's third too: and yet I would have it to say, that I writ five for two. I am not fond at all of St. James's Coffee-house, as I used to be. I hope it will mend in winter; but now they are all out of town at elections, or not come from their country houses. Yesterday I was going with Dr. Garth to dine with Charles Main, near the Tower, who has an employment there: he is of Ireland; the bishop of Clogher knows him well: an honest goodnatured fellow, a thorough hearty laugher, mightily beloved by the men of wit: his mistress is never above a cook-maid. And so, good
20 night, &c.

9. I dined to-day at sir John Stanley's; my lady Stanley is one of my favourites; I have as many here as the bishop of Killala has in Ireland. I am thinking what scurvy company I shall be to MD when I come back: they know every thing of me already: I will tell you no more, or I shall have nothing to say, no story to tell, nor any kind of thing. I was very uneasy last night with ugly, nasty, filthy wine, that turned sour on my stomach. I must go to the tavern: oh, but I told you that before. To-morrow I dine at Harley's,
30 and will finish this letter at my return; but I can write no more now, because of the archbishop: faith 'tis true; for I am going now to write to him an account of what I have done in the business with Harley: and faith, young women, I'll tell you what you must count upon, that I never will write one word on the third side in these long letters.

10. Poor MD's letter was lying so huddled up among papers I could not find it: I mean poor Presto's letter. Well, I dined with Mr. Harley to-day, and hope some things will be done; but I must say no more: and this letter must be sent to the post-house, and not by the bell-man. I am to dine again there on Sunday next; I hope to some good issue. And so now, soon as ever I can in bed, I must begin my 6th to MD as gravely as if I had not written a word this month: fine doings, faith. Methinks I don't write as I should, because I am not in bed: see the ugly wide lines. God Almighty ever bless you, &c.

Faith, this is a whole treatise: I'll go reckon the lines on t'other sides. I've reckoned them.

Letter XXV

Chelsea, June 29, 1711.

29. Steele has had the assurance to write to me, that I would engage my lord treasurer to keep a friend of his in an employment: I believe I told you how he and Addison served me for my good offices in Steele's behalf; and I promised lord treasurer never to speak for either of them again. Sir Andrew Fountain and I dined to-day at Mrs. Vanhomrigh's. Dilly Ashe has been in town this fortnight: I saw him twice; he was four days at lord Pembroke's in the country, punning with him; his face is very well. I was this evening two or three hours at lord treasurer's, who called me doctor Thomas Swift twenty times; that's his way of teazing. I left him at nine, and got home here by ten, like a gentleman; and to-morrow morning I'll answer your little letter, sirrahs.

30. Morning. I am terrible sleepy always in a morning; I believe it is my walk over-night that disposes me to sleep; faith 'tis now striking eight, and I am but just awake.

Patrick comes early, and wakes me five or six times, but I have excuses, though I am three parts asleep. I tell him I sat up late, or slept ill in the night, and often it is a lie. I have now got little MD's letter before me, N. 16, no more, nor no less, no mistake. Dingley says, 'This letter won't be above six lines,' and I was afraid it was true, though I saw it filled on both sides. The bishop of Clogher writ me word you were in the country, and that he heard you were well: I am glad at heart MD rides, and rides, and rides. Our hot
10 weather ended in May, and all this month has been moderate: it was then so hot, I was not able to endure it; I was miserable every moment, and found myself disposed to be peevish and quarrelsome; I believe a very hot country would make me stark mad.—Yes, my head continues pretty tolerable, and I impute it all to walking. Does Stella eat fruit? I eat a little; but I always repent, and resolve against it. No, in very hot weather I always go to town by water; but I constantly walk back, for then the sun is down. And so Mrs. Proby goes with you to Wexford; she's admirable
20 company: you'll grow plaguy wise with those you frequent. Mrs. Taylor, and Mrs. Proby; take care of infection. I believe my two hundred pounds will be paid; but that Sir Alexander Cairnes is a scrupulous puppy: I left the bill with Mr. Stratford, who is to have the money. Now, madam Stella, what say you? you ride every day; I know that already, sirrah; and if you rid every day for a twelve-month, you would be still better and better. No, I hope Parvisol will not have the impudence to make you stay an hour for the money; if he does I'll un-parvisol him; pray let me know. O Lord, how
30 hasty we are, Stella can't stay writing and writing; she must write and go a cock-horse, pray now. Well; but the horses are not come to the door; the fellow can't find the bridle; your stirrup is broken; where did you put the whips, Dingley? Marg'et, where have you laid Mrs. Johnson's ribband to tie about her? reach me my mask: sup up this

before you go. So, so, a gallop, a gallop: sit fast, sirrah, and don't ride hard upon the stones.—Well, now Stella is gone, tell me, Dingley, is she a good girl? and what news is that you are to tell me?—No, I believe the box is not lost: Sterne says, it is not.—No faith, you must go to Wexford without seeing your duke of Ormond, unless you stay on purpose; perhaps you may be so wise.—I tell you this is your sixteenth letter; will you never be satisfied? No, no, I'll walk late no more; I ought less to venture it than other people, and so I was told: but I'll return to lodge in town next Thursday. When you come from Wexford I would have you send a letter of attorney to Mr. Benjamin Tooke, bookseller in London, directed to me; and he shall manage your affair. I have your parchment safely lockt up in London.—O madam Stella, welcome home; was it pleasant riding? did your horse stumble? how often did the man light to settle your stirrup? ride nine miles? faith you have galloped indeed. Well, but where's the fine thing you promised me? I have been a good boy, ask Dingley else. I believe you did not meet the fine-thing-man: faith you are a cheat. So you'll see Raymond and his wife in town. Faith that riding to Laracor gives me short sighs, as well as you. All the days I have passed here, have been dirt to those. I have been gaining enemies by the scores, and friends by the couples, which is against the rules of wisdom; because they say, one enemy can do more hurt, than ten friends can do good. But I have had my revenge at least, if I get nothing else. And so let Fate govern.——Now I think your letter is answered; and mine will be shorter than ordinary, because it must go to-day. We have had a great deal of scattering rain for some days past, yet it hardly keeps down the dust.——We have plays acted in our town, and Patrick was at one of them, oh, ho. He was damnably mauled one day when he was drunk; he was at cuffs with a brother footman, who dragged him along the floor upon his face, which lookt for a week

after as if he had the leprosy; and I was glad enough to see it. I have been ten times sending him over to you; yet now he has new cloaths, and a laced hat, which the hatter brought by his orders, and he offered to pay for the lace out of his wages.—I am to dine to-day with Dilly at Sir Andrew Fountain's, who has bought a new house, and will be weary of it in half a year. I must rise and shave, and walk to town, unless I go with the dean in his chariot at twelve, which is too late: and I have not seen that lord Peterborow yet. The
10 duke of Shrewsbury is almost well again, and will be abroad in a day or two: what care you? There it is now; you don't care for my friends. Farewell, my dearest lives, and delights, I love you better than ever, if possible, as hope saved, I do, and ever will. God Almighty bless you ever, and make us happy together; I pray for this twice every day; and I hope God will hear my poor hearty prayers.—Remember if I am used ill and ungratefully, as I have formerly been, 'tis what I am prepared for, and shall not wonder at it. Yet, I am now envied, and thought in high favour, and have every day
20 numbers of considerable men teazing me to solicit for them. And the ministry all use me perfectly well, and all that know them, say they love me. Yet I can count upon nothing, nor will, but upon MD's love and kindness.—They think me useful; they pretended they were afraid of none but me; and that they resolved to have me; they have often confessed this: yet all makes little impression on me.—Pox of these speculations! They give me the spleen; and that is a disease I was not born to. Let me alone, sirrahs, and be satisfied: I am, as long as MD and Presto are well: Little wealth, And
30 much health, And a life by stealth: that is all we want; and so farewel, dearest MD; Stella, Dingley, Presto, all together, now and for ever all together. Farewel again and again.

Letter LXIII

63. [Tuesday] London. Apr. 7. 1713

I FANCY I marked my last which I sent this day, wrong, onely 61 & it ought to be 62 I dined with Ld Tr. and thô the Business I had with him is something agst Thursday when the Parlmt is to meet, & this is Tuesday yet he put it off till to morrow, I dare not tell you what it is, lest this Lettr should miscarry or be opend; but I never saw his Fellow for Delays. the Parlnt will now certainly sitt, and every body's Expectations are ready to burst. At a Council to night, the Ld Ch Justice Parker, a Whig, spoke agst the Peace, so did Ld Chomley, anothr Whig, who is Treasur of 10 the Houshold. My Ld Keeper was this night made Ld Chancellr We hope there will soon be some Removes. ⌜Nite dee sollahs both rove Pdfr.⌝

8. Ld Chomley the right name is Cholmondeley, is this day removed from his Employmt for his last nights Speech, & Sr Richd Templ Lt Genrll, the greatest Whig in the Army is turned out, & Lt Genrll Palmes will be obliged to sell his Regimt, This is the first fruits of a Friendship I have established between two great men. I dined with Ld Tr, and did the Business I had for him to his Satisfaction, I won't tell 20 ⌜Md⌝ what is was. ⌜. . . . . for zat.⌝ the Palnt sitts to morrow for certain. Here is a Letter printed in Macartneys name vindicating himself from the murder of D. Hamilton. I must give some hints to have it answred; tis full of Lyes and will give an Opportunity of exposing that Party. To morrow will be a very important day; all the World will be at Westminster; Ld. Tr is as easy as a Lamb; They are mustring up the Proxyes of the absent Lds; but they are not in any fear, of wanting a Majority, wch Death & Accidents have increased this year. ⌜Nite Md.⌝ 30

9. I was this morning with Ld Tr to present to him a young son of the late E. of Jersey at the desire of the Widow. there

I saw the Mace & great Coach ready for Ld Tr who was going to Parlmt. Our Society met to day, but I expected the Houses would sitt longer than I cared to fast; so I dined with a Friend, and never enquired how matters went till 8 this evening, when I went to Ld Orkneys where I found Sr T. Hanmer, The Qu. delivered her Speech very well, but a little weaker in her Voice; the Crowd was vast. The Order for an Address was moved; & opposed by Ld Notingham, Halifax & Cowper—Ld Tr spoke with great spirit and Resolution; Ld Peterborow flirted agst D. Marlbrow, (who is in Germany you know) but it was in answer to one of Halifax's Impertinences. The Order for an Address passd by a Majority of 33, & the Houses rise before 6 This is the account I heard at Ld Orkneys. the Bp of Chester a high Tory was agst the Court; the Dutchess of Marlbrow sent for him some Months ago to justify her self to him in relation to the Qu.— and shewd him Letters, & told him Storyes, which the weak man believed, & was perverted. ⌜Nite Md.⌝

10. I dined with a Cousin in the City, & poor Pat Rolt was there; I have got her Rogue of a Husband leave to come to Engld from Port-mahòn; the Whigs are much down; but I reckon they have some Scheam in agitation. This Parlmt time hinders our Court meetings on Wednesdays, Thursdays, & Saterdays. I had a great deal of Business to night, which gave me a Temptation to be idle, & I lost a dozen Shillings at Ombr with Dr Prat & anothr. I have been to see tothr day the Bp Cl. & Lady, but did not see Miss. It rains every day, & yet we are all over dust. Ldy Mashams eldest boy is very ill, I doubt he will not live; & she stays at Kensington to nurse him, which vexes us all. She is so excessively fond it makes me mad; she should never leave the Qu, but leave every thing to stick to what is so much the Interest of the Publick as well as her own. This I tell her, but talk to the Winds. ⌜Nite Md.⌝

11. I dined at Ld Tr with his Saterdays company; we had

ten at Table, all Lds but my self & the Chancellr of the Exchequer. Argyle went off at 6, & was in very indifferent humor, as usuall. D. Ormd & Ld Bolingbr— were absent. I stayd till near ten, Ld Tr shewd us a small Picture enamelld work, & sett in gold, worth about 20ll, a Picture I mean of the Qu; which sh gave to Dutchess Marlbrough sett in Diamonds. When the Dutchess was leaving Engld, she took off all the Diamonds, & gave the Picture to one Mrs Higgins, (an old intriguing woman whom every body knows) bidding her to make the best of it she could. Ld Tr sent to Mrs Higgins for this Picture, & gave her a hundred Pounds for it. was ever such an ungratefull Beast as that Dutchess? or did you ever hear such a Story. I suppose the Whigs will not believe it, pray try them: takes off the diamonds & gives away the Picture to an insignificant woman as a thing of no consequences, & gives it her to sell, like a piece of old fashiond plate. Is she not a detestable Slut. ⌜Nite deelest Md.⌝

12. I went to Court to day on purpose to present Mr Berkeley one of Your Fellows of Dublin Colledge, to Ld Berkeley of Stratton. that Mr Berkeley is a very ingenious man, & great Philosophr; & I have mentiond him to all the Ministers, & given them some of his writings, & I will favor him as much as I can. This I think I am bound to in honor & Conscience, to use all my little Credit towards helping forward Men of Worth in the world. The Qu was at Chappell to day, & looks well. I dined at Ld Orkneys with D. Ormd, Ld Arran & Sr T. Hanmer. Mr St John, Secrty at Utrecht expects every moment to return there with the Ratification of the Peace. Did I tell you in my last, of Addison's Play called Cato, & that I was at the Rehearsall of it. ⌜Nite Md⌝.

13. This Morning My Friend Mr Lewis came to me, and shewed me an Order for a Warrant for the 3 vacant Deanryes, but none of them to me; this was what I always foresaw., and receive the notice of it better I believe than he

expected. I bid Mr Lewis tell Ld Tr that I took nothing ill of him, but his not giving me timely notice, as he promised to do, if he found the Qu would do nothing for me. at Noon Ld Tr hearing, I was in Mr Lewis's Office, came to me, & sd many things too long to repeat. I told him I had nothing to do but go to Ireld immediatly, for I could not with any Reputation stay longer here, unless I had somethink honorabl immediatly given to me; we dined togethr at D. Ormds, he there told me, he had stopt the Warrants for the
10 Deans, that what was done for me, might be at the same time, & he hoped to compass it to night; but I believe him not. I told the D. Ormd my Intentions; He is content Stearn should be a Bp, & I have St Patricks; but I believe nothing will come of it; for stay I will not; and so I believe for all ⌜oo . . . . oo⌝ may see me in Dublin before April ends. I am less out of humor than you would imagine, & if it were not that impertinent People will condole with me, as they used to give me Joy, I would value it less: but I will avoid company, & muster up my Baggages & send
20 them next Monday by the Carrier to Chester, and come & see my Willows, agst the Expectation of all the World. hat ⌜care I. Nite deelest logues Md⌝.

14. I dined in the City to day, and ordered a Lodging to be got ready for me agst I come to pack up my things; for I will leave this end of the Town as soon as ever the warrants for the Deanryes are out, wch are yet stopt: Ld Tr told Mr Lewis, that it should be determined to night; & so he will for a hundred nights, so he said yesterday; but I value it not. my daily journall shall be but short, till I gett into the
30 City, & then I will send away this; and follow it my self, and design to walk it all the way to Chester my man & I by 10 miles a day; it will do my Health a great deal of good; I shll do it in 14 days. ⌜Nite dee Md⌝.

15. Ld Bol— made me dine with him to day, I was as good company as ever; & told me the Qu would determine

something for me to night, the dispute is Windsor or St Patricks: I told him I would not stay for their disputes, & he thought I was in the right. Ld Masham told me that Ldy Masham is angry I have not been to see her since this Business: & desires I will come to morrow. ⌜Nite deelest Md.⌝

16. I was this noon at Ldy Mashams, who was just come from Kensington where her eldest son is sick; she said much to me of what she had talkt to Qu— & Ld Tr. the poor Ldy fell a ⌜crying⌝ shedding tears openly: She coud not bear to think of my having St Patricks &c. I was never more moved than to see so much Friendship: I woud not stay with her, but went and dined with Dr Arbuthnot, with Mr Berkeley one of your Fellows, whom I have recommended to the Dr, & to Ld Berkeley of Stratton Mr Lewis tells me, that D. Ormd has been to day with Qu— & she was content that Dr Stearn should be Bp of Dromore and I Dean of St Patricks, but then out came Ld Tr, & sd he would not be satisfied, but that I must be Prebend of Windsor, thus he perplexes things— I expect neither: but I confess, as much as I love Engld, I am so angry at this Treatmt, that if I had my Choice I would rather have St Patricks. Ldy Masham says she will speak to purpose to Qu— tomorrow. ⌜Nite . . . . . . Md.⌝

17. I went to dine at Ldy Mashams to day, & she was taken ill of a sore throat, & Aguish; She spoke to Qu last night, but had not much time. Qu— says she will determine to morrow with Ld Tr. The warrants for the Deanry's are still stopt, for fear I should be gone. Do you think any thing will be done: I don't care whethr it is or no, In the mean time I prepare for my Journy; and see no great People; nor will see Ld Tr any more, if I go. Ld Tr. tod Mr Lewis it should be done to night, so he sd 5 nights ago. ⌜Nite Md.⌝

18. This morning Mr Lewis sent me word that Ld Tr told him, Qu would determine at noon. at 3 Ld Tr sent to me to come to his Lodgings at St James's, and tod me the Qu was

at last resolved, that Dr Stearn should be Bp Dromore, and I Dean of St Patrick; and tht Stearns warrant should be drawn immediatly. You know the Deanry is in the D. Ormonds gift, but this is concerted between the Qu— Ld Tr, & D. Ormd, to make room for me. I do not know whethr it will yet be done, some unlucky Accident may yet come; neither can I feel Joy at passing my days in Ireld: and I confess I thought the Ministry would not let me go; but perhaps thy cant help it. ⌜Nite Md.⌝

10 19. I forgot to tell you that Ld Tr forced me to dine with him yesterday as usuall with his Saterday company, wch I did after frequent refusals; to day I dined with a private Friend, & was not at Court. after dinner Mr Lewis sent me a note, that Qu— staid till she knew whether duke Ormd approved of Stearn for Bp: I went this Evening and found D. Ormd. at the Cockpit, & told him, and desired he would go to Qu, and approve of Stearn. He made Objections, desired I would name any other Deanry, for he did not like Stearn, that Stearn never went to see him, that he was 20 influenced by Ar. B. Dublin &c; so all is now broken again. I sent out for Ld Tr, and told him this. He says all will do well, but I value not what he says. This Suspense vexes me worse than any thing else. ⌜Nite Md.⌝

20. I went to day by appointmt to the Cockpit, to talk with D. Ormd; he repeated the same Proposall of any othr Deanry &c. I desired, he would put me out of the Case, & do as he pleased; then with great kindness he said he would consent, but woud do it for no man alive but me &c, and he will speak to the Qu— to day or to morrow. So perhaps 30 something will come of it. I can't tell. ⌜Nite dee dee logues Md⌝.

21. D. Ormd has told Qu— he is satisfied that Stearn should be Bp, & she consents I shall be Dean, and I suppose the Warrants will be drawn in a day or two. I dined at an Ale-house with Parnel & Berkeley; for I am not in humor

to go among the Ministers, thô Ld Dartmouth invited me to dine with him to day, & Ld Tr was to be there. I sd I would if I were out of suspense. ⌜Nite sollahs Md⌝.

22. Qu says Warrant shall be drawn, but she will dispose of all in Engld & Ireld at once, to be teazed no more, this will delay it sometime; & while it is delayd I am not sure of the Qu— my Enemyes being busy; I hate their Suspense —⌜Nite sollahs.⌝

23. I dined yesterday with Genll Hamilton I forgot to tell oo: I write short Journals now, I have Eggs on the Spit. 10 This Night the Qu— has signed all the Warrants, among which Stearn is Bp of Dromore, & D. Ormd is to send over an Order for making me Dean of St Patricks. I have no doubt of him at all; I think tis now past: and I suppose Md is malicious enough to be glad & rathr have it than Wells. But you see what a Condition I am in. I thought I was to pay but 600ll for the House but Bp Cl. says 800ll. First Fruits 150ll and so with Patent, a thousand Pounds in all, so that I shall not be the better for this Deanery these 3 years. I hope in some time they will be persuaded here to 20 give me some money to pay off these debts. I must finish the Book I am writing, before I can come over; & they expect I shall pass next winter here, and then I will dun them to give me a Summ of money: however I hope to pass 4 or five months ⌜with Md, and whatever comes on it, Md's Allowance must be encreased, & shall be too fais, . . .⌝. I received ⌜oo rettle N. 39⌝ to night, just 10 weeks since I had your last. I shall write next Post to Bp Stearn; never man had so many Enemyes of Ireld as he. I carryed it with the Strongest hand possible: If he does not use me well and 30 gently in what dealings I shall have with him, he will be the most ungratefull of Mankind. A.Bp York, my mortall Enemy, has sent by a third hand that he would be glad to see me; Shall I see him or not?—I hope to be over in a Month; & that ⌜Md⌝ with their Raillery, will be mistaken

tht I shall make it 3 years. I will answr oor Rettle soon; but no more Journals: I shall be very busy. Short letters from henceforward. I shall not part with Laracor: that is all I have to live on; except the Deanry be worth more than 400ll a year; is it? if it be, the over-plus shall be divided ⌜. . . . . besides te usuall . . . .⌝ Pray write to me a good humored Lettr immediatly, let it be ever so short. This Affair was carryed with great difficulty, wch vexes me, but they say here tis much to my Reputation, that I have made a Bp in spight of all the Wor[l]d, to get the best Deanry in Ireld. ⌜Nite dee sollahs.⌝

24. I forgot to tell you, I had Stearns Lettr yesterday in answr to mine. ⌜oo performd oor Commission well, dood Dallars both.⌝ I made mistakes the 3 last days and am forced to alter the Numbr. I dined in the City to day with my Printer, and came home early; & am going to busy with my Work. I will send this to morrow, & I suppose the warrants will go then. I wrote to Dr Coghill to take care of passing my Patent, & to Parvisol to attend him with money, if he has any; or to borrow some where he can. ⌜Nite Md⌝—

25. Morn. I know not whethr my Warrant be yet ready from D. Ormd; I suppose it will by to night; I am going abroad, & will keep this unsealed till I know whethr all be finisht: ⌜mollow Sollahs.⌝ ——I had this Letter all day in my Pocket, waiting till I heard the Warrants were gone over. Mr Lewis sent to Southwells Clerk at 10, & he sd the Bp Killaloo had desired they shoud be stoppt till next post, he sent again that Bp Killaloo's Business had nothing to do with ours; then I went my self; but it was past 11, & asked the Reason. Killaloo is removed to Rapho, and he has a mind to have an Order for the Rents of Rapho that have fallen since the Vacancy, & he would have all stop till he has got that. a pretty Request; but the Clerk at Mr Lewis's message sent the Warrants for Stearn & me. but it was then too late

to send this, wch fretts me heartily, ⌜tht Md shoud not have Intelligence first from Pdfr⌝. I think to take a hundred Pound a year out of the Deanry, & divide it ⌜between Md & Pr. & so be one year longer be paying te Debt, but we'll talk of zis hen I come over, so Nite dee sollahs lele⌝—

26. I was at Court to day; & a thousand People gave me joy, so I ran out. I dined with Ldy Orkney—Yesterday I dined with Ld Treasur & his Saterday People as usuall, & was bedean'd—A.B. York says he will never more speak agst me—Pray see that Parvisol stirs about getting my Patent. I have given Took Dd's note to prove she is alive. I'⌜ll answer Md Rettle anoddle time—Nite.⌝ 10

27. Nothing new to day. I dined with Tom Harley &c. I'll seal up this to night. pray write soon.—

⌜. . . . . Md Md FW FW FW Me Me Me Lele lele⌝

Address: To Mrs Dingley at her
Lodgings over against St. Mary's
Church near Capel-street
Ireland Dublin

CORRESPONDENCE

Letter to Pope, 29 Sept. 1725

I CANNOT guess the reason of Mr. Stopford's management, but impute it at a venture to either haste or bashfulness, in the latter of which he is excessive to a fault, although he had already gone the tour of Italy and France to harden himself. Perhaps this second journey, and for a longer time, may amend him. He treated you just as he did Lord Carteret, to whom I recommended him.

My letter you saw to Lord Bolinbroke has shown you the situation I am in, and the company I keep, if I do not forget
10 some of its contents, but I am now returning to the noble scene of Dublin, into the *grand monde,* for fear of burying my parts, to signalise myself among curates and vicars, and correct all corruptions crept in relating to the weight of bread and butter, through those dominions where I govern. I have employed my time, besides ditching, in finishing, correcting, amending, and transcribing my Travels, in four parts complete, newly augmented, and intended for the press, when the world shall deserve them, or rather when a printer shall be found brave enough to venture his ears.
20 I like the scheme of our meeting after distresses and dispersions; but the chief end I propose to myself in all my labours is to vex the world rather than divert it; and if I could compass that design, without hurting my own person or fortune, I would be the most indefatigable writer you have ever seen, without reading. I am exceedingly pleased that you have done with translations. Lord Treasurer Oxford often lamented that a rascally world should lay you under a necessity of mis-employing your genius for so long a time. But since you will now be so much better employed,
30 when you think of the world give it one lash the more at my request. I have ever hated all nations, professions, and

communities, and all my love is toward individuals: for instance, I hate the tribe of lawyers, but I love Counsellor Such-a-one, and Judge Such-a-one: so with physicians—I will not speak of my own trade—soldiers, English, Scotch, French, and the rest. But principally I hate and detest that animal called man, although I heartily love John, Peter, Thomas, and so forth. This is the system upon which I have governed myself many years, but do not tell, and so I shall go on till I have done with them. I have got materials toward a treatise, proving the falsity of that definition *animal rationale,* and 10 to show it would be only *rationis capax.* Upon this great foundation of misanthropy, though not in Timon's manner, the whole building of my travels is erected; and I never will have peace of mind till all honest men are of my opinion. By consequence you are to embrace it immediately, and procure that all who deserve my esteem may do so too. The matter is so clear that it will admit of no dispute; nay, I will hold a hundred pounds that you and I agree in the point.

I did not know your Odyssey was finished, being yet in the country, which I shall leave in three days. I shall thank 20 you kindly for the present, but shall like it three-fourths the less, from the mixture you mention of another hand; however, I am glad you saved yourself so much drudgery. I have long been told by Mr. Ford of your great achievements in building and planting, and especially of your subterranean passage to your garden, whereby you turned a blunder into a beauty, which is a piece of *ars poetica.*

I have almost done with harridans, and shall soon become old enough to fall in love with girls of fourteen. The lady whom you describe to live at court, to be deaf, and no party 30 woman, I take to be mythology, but know not how to moralize it. She cannot be Mercy, for Mercy is neither deaf, nor lives at court. Justice is blind, and perhaps deaf, but neither is she a Court lady. Fortune is both blind and deaf, and a Court lady, but then she is a most damnable party woman, and will never make me easy, as you promise. It must be Riches, which answers all your description. I am glad she visits you, but my voice is so weak that I doubt she will never hear me.

Mr. Lewis sent me an account of Dr. Arbuthnot's illness, which is a very sensible affliction to me, who, by living so long out of the world, have lost that hardness of heart contracted by years and general conversation. I am daily losing friends, and neither seeking nor getting others. Oh! if the world had but a dozen Arbuthnots in it, I would burn my Travels. But, however, he is not without fault. There is a passage in Bede highly commending the piety and learning of the Irish in that age, where, after abundance of praises, he overthrows them all, by lamenting that, alas! they kept Easter at a wrong time of the year. So our Doctor has every quality and virtue that can make a man amiable or useful; but, alas! he has a sort of slouch in his walk. I pray God protect him, for he is an excellent Christian, though not a Catholic, and as fit a man either to live or die as ever I knew.

I hear nothing of our friend Gay, but I find the Court keeps him at hard meat. I advised him to come over here with a Lord Lieutenant. Mr. Tickell is in a very good office. I have not seen Philips, though formerly we were so intimate. He has got nothing and by what I find will get nothing, though he writes little flams, as Lord Leicester called those sorts of verses, on Miss Carteret. It is remarkable, and deserves recording that a Dublin blacksmith, a great poet, has imitated his manner in a poem to the same Miss. Philips is a complainer, and on this occasion I told Lord Carteret that complainers never succeed at Court, though railers do.

Are you altogether a country gentleman, that I must address to you out of London, to the hazard of your losing this precious letter, which I will now conclude, although so much paper is left. I have an ill name, and therefore shall not subscribe it, but you will guess it comes from one who esteems and loves you about half as much as you deserve, I mean as much as he can.

I am in great concern, at what I am just told is in some of the newspapers, that Lord Bolinbroke is much hurt by a fall in hunting. I am glad he has so much youth and vigour left, of which he has not been thrifty, but I wonder he has no more discretion.

Letter to Motte, 28 Dec. 1727

I HAD yours of the 16th from Mr. Hyde, and desire that henceforth you will write directly to me, without scrupling 10 to load me with the postage. My head is so confused with the returns of my deafness to a very great degree—which left me after a fortnight, and then returned with more violence—that I am in an ill way to answer a letter which requires some thinking.

As to having cuts in Gulliver's Travels, you will consider how much it will raise the price of the book. The world glutted itself with that book at first, and now it will go off but soberly; but I suppose will not be soon worn out. The part of the little men will bear cuts much better than that 20 of the great. I have not the book by me, but will speak by memory. Gulliver in his carriage to the metropolis, his extinguishing the fire, the ladies in their coaches driving about his table, his rising up out of his carriage when he is fastened to his horse, his drawing the fleet, the troop upon his handkerchief, the army marching between his legs, his hat drawn by eight horses, seem the fittest to be represented, and perhaps two adventures may be sometimes put in one print.

It is difficult to do anything in the great men, because 30 Gulliver makes so diminutive a figure, and he is but one in the whole kingdom. Among some cuts I bought in London, he is shown taken out of the bowl of cream; but the hand that holds him hides the whole body. He would appear best wedged in the marrow-bone up to the middle, or in the monkey's arms upon the roof, or left upon the ridge, and the footman on the ladder going to relieve him, or fighting with the rats on the farmer's bed, or in the spaniel's mouth, which being described as a small dog, he might look as large as a duck in one of ours. One of the best would be, I think, 10 to see his chest just falling into the sea, while three eagles are quarreling with one another; or the monkey hauling him out of his box. Mr. Wootton, the painter who draws landscapes and horses, told Mr. Pope and me that the graver did wrong in not making the big folks bear something [large], and enormous in their shapes, for, as drawn by those gravers, they look only like common human creatures. Gulliver being alone, and so little, cannot make the contrast appear.

The Flying Island might be drawn at large as described in 20 the book, and Gulliver drawing up into it, and some fellows with flappers. I know not what to do with the Projectors. Nor what figure the Island of Ghosts would make, or any passage related in it, because I do not well remember it.

The Country of Horses, I think, would furnish many. Gulliver brought to be compared with the Yahoos; the family at dinner and he waiting; the grand council of horses, assembled, sitting, one of them standing with a hoof extended, as if he were speaking; the she-Yahoos embracing Gulliver in the river, who turns away his head in disgust; 30 the Yahoos got into a tree, to infest him under it; the Yahoos drawing carriages, and driven by a horse with a whip in his hoof. I can think of no more, but Mr. Gay will advise you, and carry you to Mr. Wootton and some other skilful people.

As to the poetical volume of Miscellany, I believe five

parts in six, at least, are mine. Our two friends, you know, have printed their works already, and we could expect nothing but slight loose papers. There is all the poetry I ever writ worth printing. Mr. Pope rejected some I sent him, for I desired him to be as severe as possible, and I will take his judgement. He writ to me, that he intended a pleasant discourse on the subject of poetry should be printed before the volume, and says that discourse is ready. . . . I am as weary with writing as I fear you will be with reading. I am, Yours, &c. 10

Letter to Arbuthnot, Nov. 1734

My dear Friends,

I never once suspected your forgetfulness or want of friendship, but very often dreaded your want of health, to which alone I imputed every delay longer than ordinary in hearing from you. I should be very ungrateful, indeed, if I acted otherwise to you, who are pleased to take such generous constant care of my health, my interests, and my reputation, who represented me so favourably to that blessed Queen your mistress, as well as to her Ministers, and to all your friends. The letters you mention, which I did not answer, 20 I cannot find, and yet I have all that ever came from you, for I constantly endorse yours and those of a few other friends, and date them; only if there be anything particular, though of no consequence, when I go to the country I send them to some friends among other papers for fear of accidents in my absence. I thank you kindly for your favour to the young man who was bred in my choir. The people of skill in music represent him to me as a lad of virtue, and hopeful and endeavouring in his way. It is your own fault if I give you trouble, because you never refused me anything 30 in your life.

You tear my heart with the ill account of your health;

yet if it should please God to call you away before me, I should not pity you in the least, except on the account of what pains you might feel before you passed into a better life. I should pity none but your friends, and among them chiefly myself, although I never can hope to have health enough to leave this country till I leave the world. I do not know among mankind any person more prepared to depart from us than yourself, not even the Bishop of Marseilles, if he be still alive; for among all your qualities that have
10 procured you the love and esteem of the world, I ever most valued your moral and Christian virtues, which were not the product of years or sickness, but of reason and religion, as I can witness after above five-and-twenty years' acquaintance. I except only the too little care of your fortune; upon which I have been so free as sometimes to examine and to chide you, and the consequence of which hath been to confine you to London, when you are under a disorder for which I am told, and know, that the clear air of the country is necessary.

20 The great reason that hinders my journey to England, is the same that drives you from Highgate. I am not in circumstances to keep horses and servants in London. My revenues by the miserable oppressions of this kingdom are sunk three hundred pounds a year, for tithes are become a drug, and I have but little rents from the deanery lands, which are my only sure payments. I have here a large convenient house; I live at two-thirds cheaper here than I could there; I drink a bottle of French wine myself every day, though I love it not, but it is the only thing that keeps me
30 out of pain; I ride every fair day a dozen miles, on a large strand or turnpike roads. You in London have no such advantages. I can buy a chicken for a groat, and entertain three or four friends, with as many dishes, and two or three bottles of French wine, for ten shillings. When I dine alone, my pint and chicken with the appendixes cost me about

fifteen pence. I am thrifty in everything but wine, of which though I be not a constant housekeeper, I spend between five and six hogshead a year. When I ride to a friend a few miles off, if he be not richer than I, I carry my bottle, my bread and chicken, that he may be no loser.

I talk thus foolishly to let you know the reasons which, joined to my ill-health, make it impossible for me to see you and my other friends; and perhaps this domestic tattle may excuse me and amuse you. I could not live with my Lord Bolinbroke or Mr. Pope: they are both too temperate and 10 too wise for me, and too profound and too poor. And how could I afford horses? And how could I ride over their cursed roads in winter, and be turned into a ditch by every carter or hackney-coach? Every parish minister of this city is governor of all carriages, and so are the two Deans, and every carrier should make way for us at their peril. Therefore, like Caesar, I will be one of the first here rather than the last among you. I forget that I am so near the bottom. I am now with one of my Prebendaries, five miles in the country, for five days. I brought with me eight bottles of 20 wine, with bread and meat for three days, which is my club; he is a bachelor, with three hundred pounds a year. May God preserve you, my dear friend.

Entirely yours,
J. Swift.

NOTES

APPRECIATIONS

pp. xvii–xxiii. Dr. Arbuthnot, Gay, and Pope were Swift's closest friends at the time when he returned to London in 1726 to arrange for the publication of *Gulliver's Travels.* Their letters show something of the immediate response to the book and the sort of pleasure it gave to its first readers.

p. xxiii. Lord Bathurst, one of the twelve new Tory peers created by Queen Anne in 1712 and a friend of Swift and Pope later, and admirer of their writings.

p. xxv. John Boyle, fifth Earl of Orrery, who succeeded to his Irish estate in 1731 at the age of 24, and cultivated Swift's friendship during his last years. His rather patronizing *Remarks on the Life and Writings of Swift,* 1752, was the first of many books to exploit the oddities and mysteries of Swift's character, and to provoke angry comments from Swift's friends. But in his comments on Swift's style in prose and verse and on his writings on behalf of Ireland he is the first to express a view of Swift's position in literature and politics, which would have been then widely accepted. *Observations upon Lord Orrery's Remarks,* by Swift's friend Patrick Delany, was the first reply to Orrery's criticisms. His final summing up—here quoted—was reprinted by Dr. Johnson in his *Life of Swift,* to balance any unfairness in his own remarks on Swift's character: in the passage given here, however, Johnson shows his recognition of Swift's powers as a political writer and his appreciation of the particular qualities of his style.

p. xxx. Sir Walter Scott prefixed a Life of Swift to his edition of Swift's *Works,* with notes in 19 vols, 1814.

p. xxxii. Hazlitt discusses Swift in the Sixth of his *Lectures on the English Poets,* 1818, recognizing his place in the great tradition of European satire from Rabelais to Voltaire.

p. xxxvii. David Nichol Smith gives an account of Swift's long and strenuous course of reading in preparation for the writing of *A Tale of a Tub,* the work of a brilliant wit, who has first mastered much heterogeneous learning, which is put to splendid use for satiric purposes. He also first printed Swift's Letters to his friend Charles Ford, which provided much fresh information about the writing of *Gulliver's Travels,* as shown in the passage here quoted.

PROSE

p. 2. BATTLE OF THE BOOKS, first published in 1704, probably written about 1697 concerning the dispute over Ancient and Modern Learning, in which Swift came to the defence of Sir William Temple and Charles Boyle, who had been roughly handled by the great classical scholar Dr. Bentley. The Preface of the Author shows the mastery Swift had already gained in using the weapons of satire. His story of the encounter of the spider and the bee is an imitation of an Aesop fable, and reminds us very appropriately of a sentence in Temple's essay *On Poetry*, 1696: '[Bees] must range through Fields, as well as Gardens, chuse such flowers as they please, and by Proprieties and Scents they only know and distinguish: They must work up their Cells with admirable Art, extract their Honey with infinite Labour, and sever it from the Wax, with such Distinction and Choice, as belongs to none but themselves to perform and judge.' Some of his readers would also remember a passage from Bacon's *Novum Organum*: 'The men of experiment are like the ant; they only collect and use; the reasoners resemble spiders, who make cobwebs out of their own substance. But the bee takes a middle course, it gathers its material from the flowers of the garden and of the field, but transforms and digests it by a power of its own. Not unlike this is the true business of philosophy.' In a later stage of the battle between the Ancients and the moderns in the nineteenth century, Matthew Arnold took over Swift's phrase 'sweetness and light' and used it in his battle with the enemies of culture.

p. 7. A TALE OF A TUB: 'A Digression on Madness'.

p. 9, *l.* 2. *How shrunk is every Thing*, cf. Bacon, *Essayes*, 'Of Truth': 'if there were taken out of Mens Mindes, Vaine Opinions, Flattering Hopes, False valuations, Imaginations as one would, and the like; but it would leave the Mindes, of a Number of Men, poor shrunken Things; . . .'

p. 11, *l.* 16. *Curtius* who according to legend sacrificed himself by leaping into the deep gulf which had opened in the forum, since it could only be closed by throwing into it Rome's most valuable possession.

p. 11, *l.* 16. *Empedocles* was said to have cast himself into the crater of Aetna, so that it might be believed that he had been translated to heaven. But the volcano cast forth his brazen sandals, thus revealing the manner of his death.

p. 11, *ll.* 27–28. *Sir Edward Seymour . . . John How, Esq.* leading

Tory members of the House of Commons. In 1701 John Bowls went mad.

p. 13, *l.* 30. *Warwick-Lane,* where the Royal College of Physicians was started in 1674.

p. 15. Meditation upon a Broom-stick. Written in 1704 and first printed in *Miscellanies,* 1711. The occasion is described by Thomas Sheridan in his *Life of Swift* as follows:

'In the yearly visits which he made to London, during his stay there, he passed much of his time at Lord Berkeley's, officiating as chaplain to the family, and attending Lady Berkeley in her private devotions. After which, the doctor, by her desire, used to read to her some moral or religious discourse. The countess had at this time taken a great liking to Mr. Boyle's Meditations, and was determined to go through them in that manner; but as Swift had by no means the same relish for that kind of writing which her ladyship had, he soon grew weary of the task. . . . The next time he was employed in reading one of these Meditations, he took an opportunity of conveying away the book, and dexterously inserted a leaf, on which he had written his own "Meditation on a Broomstick"; after which, he took care to have the book restored to its proper place, and in his next attendance on my lady, when he was desired to proceed to the next Meditation, Swift . . . with an inflexible gravity of countenance, proceeded to read the Meditation, in the same solemn tone he had used in delivering the former. . . . Soon after, some company coming in, Swift pretended business, and withdrew, foreseeing what was to follow. Lady Berkeley, full of the subject, soon entered upon the praises of those heavenly Meditations of Mr. Boyle. "But," said she, "the doctor has been just reading one to me, which has surprised me more than all the rest . . . I mean, that excellent Meditation on a Broomstick." The company looked at each other with some surprise, and could scarce refrain from laughing. . . . One of them opened the book, and found it there indeed, but in Swift's handwriting; upon which a general burst of laughter ensued; and my lady, when the first surprise was over, enjoyed the joke as much as any of them, saying, "What a vile trick that rogue played me. But it is his way, he never balks his humour in any thing." The affair ended in a great deal of harmless mirth, and Swift, you may be sure, was not asked to proceed any farther in the Meditations.'[1]

[1] See Swift's *Works,* re-edited by John Nichols, vol. i, 1812, pp. 113–14.

p. 16. An Argument, etc. A parody of formal logical reasoning in which Swift ironically attacks the Deists and the free-thinkers, who claim that their position is based upon reason; and those nonconformists and Anglicans who were opposed to the 'Test Act', by which the holders of civil and political offices were restricted to those who received the sacraments as members of the Church of England.

p. 16, *l.* 20. The *Union,* between England and Scotland in 1707, which had been opposed in many quarters. Swift was always prejudiced against the Scots, and feared that the Union would weaken the position of the Established Church.

p. 17, *l.* 32. *Trinitarians,* referring to attacks on the orthodox doctrine of the Trinity.

p. 18, *l.* 28. *Cavil,* frivolous objection.

p. 19, *l.* 33. *Sorites,* the use of this technical term in logic, meaning a chain of syllogisms, should remind us that Swift's *Argument* is a parody of formal logic.

p. 21. A Letter to a Young Gentleman, lately entered into Holy Orders. Though Swift has designed this letter as if written by 'a Person of Quality', a man of good taste and worldly wisdom, it contains not only his own views on the clear simple style he admired both in writing and in preaching; but it is written evidently out of his own experience as a preacher, and as a writer whose pamphlets were intended to reach a wide audience.

p. 21, *l.* 30. *Lord Falkland,* Lucius Cary, 2nd Viscount, killed at the battle of Newbury in 1643, a man of the highest reputation and promise as a scholar and a leader of the moderate party; one or two speeches printed in his lifetime, and afterwards his Discourse of Infallibility reprinted several times.

p. 24, *l.* 17. *For my Part,* &c. Note here the way in which Swift makes use of the character of 'a Person of Quality' which he has assumed, to put himself in an 'impartial position' between the young clergyman he is addressing and 'those Gentlemen, you call the Free-Thinkers'.

p. 24. A Letter to a Young Lady on her Marriage, 1723. Written to Deborah Staunton who was marrying one of Swift's friends, John Rochfort, to welcome her into their circle with advice and offers of his help. An example of Swift's prose at the height of his powers, as he condescends to open his whole mind to this young lady on the subject of the behaviour and education of a gentlewoman.

p. 26, *l.* 29. *Billingsgate,* the fishmarket where the fishwomen were famous from the seventeenth century for the richness of their abusive language.

p. 31. DRAPIER'S LETTER TO LORD MOLESWORTH. After writing the four *Drapier Letters* to persuade the people of Ireland to refuse Wood's copper coinage, Swift addressed this justification of his activities to Lord Molesworth, whose loyalty to George I had been rewarded by a peerage in 1719, but whose *Considerations for promoting Agriculture in Ireland,* 1723, had proved his concern with the state of Ireland. Here Swift cleverly uses his disguise and the language of his trade to 'give some little account of my self'.

GULLIVER'S TRAVELS

p. 35. The Letter from Capt. Gulliver, dated 12 Apr. 1727, was first printed as a preface to the Dublin edition of Swift's *Works,* vol. iii, in 1735, and was probably written about 1733 for this purpose. It was in Oct. 1733 that he wrote to Ford to ask him to supply the original text of the 'mangled and murdered pages'; and in the first paragraph of Gulliver's Letter, he refers to several passages, where 'you have either omitted some material Circumstances, or minced or changed them in such a Manner, that I do hardly know mine own Works'.

p. 35, *l.* 7. *A Voyage round the World.* This is Swift's way of acknowledging his imitation of Dampier's well-known book in the general structure he used for Gulliver's four voyages.

p. 36, *l.* 4. *so many Years ago.* Gulliver dated his stay with the Houyhnhnms from May 1711 till Feb. 1715.

p. 36, *l.* 30. *Smithfield,* the London cattle market, where heretics and their books were burnt.

p. 37, *ll.* 12–13. *Keys and . . . Second Parts.* e.g. *A Key, being Observations and Explanatory Notes upon the Travels of Lemuel Gulliver* by Signor Corolini, 1726; and *Travels by Captain Lemuel Gulliver,* vol. iii, 1727.

p. 37, *l.* 22. *confound the Times . . . and the Dates,* a recognition by the author of the confusion in the dating of Gulliver's different voyages and the periods between them, which, however, was not altogether removed by the changes made in 1735. See A. E. Case, *Four Essays on Gulliver's Travels,* Princeton, 1945, pp. 61 f.

p. 37, *l.* 28. *second Edition.* A second edition, corrected, was published in 1727; but the corrections were limited to the removal of a number of minor errors which had been noted by Charles Ford.

p. 39, *l.* 13. *visionary schemes,* cf. *A Modest Proposal,* p. 9, l. 1. 'having been wearied out for many Years with offering vain, idle, visionary Thoughts . . .'. As modern critics have been so concerned to warn us against believing that Gulliver's opinions were shared by Swift, it may be pertinent to quote the statement at the end of *A Proposal for Giving Badges to Beggars,* 1737, which is signed J. Swift: 'I had some other Thoughts to offer upon this Subject. But, as I am a Desponder in my Nature, and have tolerably well discovered the Disposition of our People, who never will move a Step towards easing themselves from any one single Grievance; it will be thought, that I have already said too much, and to little or no Purpose; which hath often been the Fate, or Fortune of the Writer.'

p. 39, *l.* 14. *Gulliver.* An actual family name in Banbury, where Swift may well have first noticed it, and perhaps liked the sound of it, as suitable for his honest and naïve traveller.

p. 41, *l.* 7. *at fourteen years old.* Swift entered Trinity College, Dublin, at that age.

p. 41, *l.* 20. *Leyden.* The university was famous for the study of medicine.

p. 41, *l.* 26. *the Levant,* i.e. the Eastern Mediterranean.

p. 41, *l.* 29. *Old Jury,* once the Jewish quarter of the City of London.

p. 42, *l.* 29. *Van Diemen's Land,* Tasmania, then thought to be a part of the Australian mainland. Swift was careful to place all the new countries which Gulliver discovered in those parts of the world which still remained unknown and unmapped.

p. 44, *l.* 6. *six Inches high.* Swift uses a simple scale by making the size of everything in Lilliput equal in inches to our sizes in feet; reversed the scale in Brobdingnag.

p. 44, *l.* 17. *Hekinah Degul.* Many attempts have been made to explain Swift's method of inventing languages; but it may be only a further development of the word games and Anglo-Latin tricks he often indulged in. Ingenious interpretations have been suggested by Emil Pons, *Rabelais et Swift a propos du Lilliputien,* Paris, 1936; and P. Odell Clark, *A Gulliver Dictionary,* S.P., 1953, vol. l, p. 592.

p. 50, *l.* 33. *an ancient Temple.* Swift may have had in mind Westminster Hall, where Charles I had been condemned to death.

Part II, Chapters 6 and 7

p. 53, *l.* 14. *Consorts*, concerts made by a company of musicians.

p. 55, *l.* 12. *Plantations*, colonies.

p. 55, *l.* 22. *highest Court of Judicature*, the House of Lords as the final Court of Appeal.

p. 58, *l.* 29. *Issues*, i.e. of bills of exchange, bonds, coinage, &c.

p. 59, *l.* 5. *Generals richer than Kings*. Swift could never refrain from a thrust at the Duke of Marlborough.

p. 59, *l.* 9. *a standing Army in the midst of Peace*, then generally opposed by the Tories.

p. 60, *l.* 17. *Grildrig*, mannikin.

p. 61, *l.* 25. *Dionysius Halicarnassensis*, a Greek historian, who lived under Augustus, at Rome, and devoted himself with laudable partiality to a study of the early history of his adopted country.

p. 62, *l.* 11. *Invention to make a certain Powder*. In the controversy between the Ancients and the Moderns one of the claims for the superiority of the latter was based on their dis covery of gunpowder.

p. 66, *l.* 3. *the usual Topicks of European Moralists*, which Swift is always ready to ridicule; here diverting himself by supposing that the giant Brobdingnagians likewise complain of the degeneracy of Nature in these later times, and argue that 'there must have been Giants in former Ages'.

p. 66, *l.* 35. *Army made up of Tradesmen and Farmers*, not a standing army of mercenaries.

Part III, Chapter 3

p. 68, *l.* 10. *Flying Island*. See M. Nicolson and N. Mohler, *The Scientific Background of the Voyage to Laputa*: Annals of Science, 1937, ii, 299, 405. From Kepler to Defoe, voyages to the moon had involved flying machines.

p. 69, *l.* 2. *Astronomers Cave*, probably suggested by the well-known cave (with 170 descending steps) in the Observatory at Paris.

p. 69, *l.* 5. *Adamant*, shining and magnetic, like a diamond.

p. 69, *l.* 9. *Loadstone*. This account based on Gilbert's 'tipping needle' and 'terrella' in his great work on Magnetism, and parodies papers on magnetical experiments in the *Philosophical Transactions of the Royal Society* from 1701 on.

p. 71, *ll.* 19–20. *satellites of Mars*. Jupiter's four and Saturn's five satellites were known. The Laputan discovery of two for Mars, which Swift seems to have worked out according to Kepler's laws, anticipated the observation of 1877.

p. 71, *l.* 33. *theory of comets.* Edmond Halley's *Astronomiae Cometicae Synopsis* had appeared in 1705.

Part IV, Chapter 10

p. 73. A chapter in which Swift seems to be trying to convince his readers that Gulliver had finally discovered his Utopia in the land of the Houyhnhnms, where he could enjoy 'perfect Health of Body and Tranquillity of Mind'.

p. 73, *l.* 23. *economy,* in the simplest sense of domestic arrangements.

p. 79, *l.* 1. *think with temper,* temperately, without violent emotions.

p. 80, *l.* 1. *artificially,* skilfully contrived.

THE INTELLIGENCER, NO. III

p. 82. Swift and Sheridan started a small weekly paper in Dublin on 11 May 1728, and for the third number Swift wrote this defence of Gay's *Beggar's Opera,* which had had such a great success in London in the previous winter, and in Dublin during the spring. It gave him an admirable opportunity to state his views on humour and satire, and in defending Gay to justify his own intentions in the writing of *Gulliver's Travels.*

p. 82, *l.* 15. *Sir William Temple,* who had discussed humour in his essay *On Poetry,* 1690.

p. 82, *l.* 22. *Rabelais, Cervantes,* by whose side Swift places himself in the great European tradition of 'true Humour'.

A MODEST PROPOSAL

p. 84. Printed at the end of Oct. 1729, in Dublin, and immediately reprinted in London. It appeared anonymously, but in the same format as the *Drapier Letters,* and it was advertised in the *Dublin Intelligence* for 8 Nov., as 'said to be written by D—— S——'. It was put forth among the many proposals for remedying the ills of Ireland, and addressed directly to an Irish audience. In its form it imitates the serious proposals, giving full details of the scheme and gravely setting down the advantages and dealing with possible objections. The author finally concludes that there is no other way so sure to provide what is necessary—the public good of the country, 'by advancing Trade, providing for Infants, relieving the Poor, and giving some Pleasure to the Rich'.

p. 84, *l.* 31. *beggars,* estimated by Arthur Dobbs at this time to number 34,425. Swift put forward another proposal in 1737 dealing with Beggars, in which he suggested that those in genuine want should be provided with badges by the parish they belonged to, where alone they would receive help.

p. 85, *l.* 6. *fight for the Pretender in Spain,* Irish Catholics had been recruited for service in the Spanish army, in an attempt to restore the Pretender in 1719.

p. 85, *l.* 11. *present deplorable state of the Kingdom,* 'three terrible years' dearth of corn' which Swift had mentioned in his letter to Pope, 11 Aug. 1729. This had driven many to emigrate to the West Indies.

p. 86, *l.* 31. *the county of Cavan,* of which Swift seems to have had a poor opinion; cf. his verses to Sheridan, who later had a school there:

> You live among ill folks in a dunghill
> You never have an old friend at Cavan.

p. 87, *l.* 21. *our Savages,* the native Irish.

p. 88, *l.* 1. *proper for Landlords,* whom Swift regarded as responsible, in large part, for Ireland's wretched condition, as absentee landlords who did nothing to improve the condition of their tenants, or the state of agriculture.

p. 88, *l.* 14. *pay Tithes against their conscience,* the Scottish settlers, being Presbyterians and Calvinists, objected against supporting the Established Episcopal Church.

p. 88, *l.* 17. *lyable to distress,* subject to seizure for debt.

p. 90, *l.* 12. *other Expedients,* many of which Swift had himself proposed in vain in his earlier tracts, e.g. *A Proposal for the Universal Use of Irish Manufactures etc.,* 1720.

p. 91, *l.* 6. *no Danger in disobliging England,* in Swift's eyes the chief cause of the miseries of Ireland, owing to the restrictions imposed on Irish trade.

POEMS

p. 93. On Sir William Temple's late Illness, the last of the poems written during Swift's earlier stay at Moor Park, in which he celebrates his escape from the power of the Muse he had vainly invoked in his attempts at Pindarics and panegyric, and refuses to have anything more to do with romantic poetry, enchantments, or visionary powers. The result may be seen in the two following poems.

p. 94. A DESCRIPTION OF THE MORNING, printed in *The Tatler*, no. 9, 30 Apr. 1709, with a comment by Steele, introducing it as something 'perfectly new' to expose the current taste for pastoral—Sonnets on Phillis and Chloris, and Fantastical Descriptions—'He never forms Fields, or Nymphs, or Groves, where they are not, but makes the Incidents just as they really appear. . . . They are a Description of the Morning, but of the Morning in Town'.

p. 94, *l.* 10. *Kennel-edge*, ditch at the side of the street, which serves as a drain; cf. next poem ll. 53 f.

p. 94, *ll.* 11, 14. *Smallcoal-Man . . . brickdust Moll*, street vendors.

p. 94, *l.* 17. *Bailiffs*, waiting to arrest debtors.

p. 95. A CITY SHOWER, printed in *The Tatler*, no. 238, 17 Oct. 1710. Swift later added, in 1727, to the title 'In Imitation of Virgil's *Georg*'. Mentions writing it in the *Journal to Stella*, and when it appeared says: 'They say 'tis the best thing I ever writ, and I think so too.' Steele introduced it with a comment on the descriptions of storms at sea in the ancient poets, and Virgil's Land-Shower, which had frequently been imitated by recent pastoral poets 'generally filled with the Lowings of Oxen, and the Bleatings of Sheep, and very often embellished with a Rainbow'. But the Description of a City Shower is treated 'after a Manner that no other Author has done, and better than any other can do'.

p. 95, *l.* 3. *depends*, is impending.

p. 95, *l.* 5. *the Sink*, cf. *Journal to Stella*, 8 Nov. 1710: 'I am almost stunk out of this [lodging] with the sink, and it helps me to verses in my Shower.'

p. 95, *l.* 10. *Aches*, pronounced then as a dissyllable, *aitches*.

p. 95, *l.* 26. *'Twas doubtful which was Rain*, a parody of Garth's *Dispensary* (v. 176):

> 'Tis doubtful which is Sea, and which is Sky.'

p. 95, *l.* 29. *His only Coat*, &c., altered in 1735 to

> Sole Coat, where Dust cemented by the Rain
> Erects the Nap, and leaves a cloudy Stain.

p. 96, *l.* 41. *Triumphant Tories and desponding Whigs,* Godolphin, the Lord Treasurer since the Queen's accession in 1702, had been dismissed from office on 8 Aug. 1710; and the Tories were gaining power under the new Treasurer, Harley, with whom Swift was already associated.

p. 96, *l.* 60. *Holborn-Bridge,* where the Fleet was still a navigable stream.

p. 96, *l.* 61. *Sweepings from Butchers Stalls,* &c. See note added in 1735: 'These three last lines were intended against that licentious Manner of modern Poets, in making three Rhimes together, which they call *Triplets*; and the last of the three, was two or sometimes more Syllables longer, called an Alexandrian. These Triplets and Alexandrians were brought in by Dryden, and other poets in the reign of Charles II. They were the mere Effect of Haste, Idleness, and Want of Money; and have been wholly avoided by the best Poets, since these verses were written.'

p. 97. A SATIRICAL ELEGY. The Duke died on 16 June 1722. Swift had first dealt with Marlborough in *The Examiner,* no. 16, 23 Nov. 1710, where he defends the Tories against the charge of ingratitude to the Duke for his most eminent services to his country, not to be equalled in history. He had satirized him before in verse, in *The Fable of Midas,* 1711; and had attacked him also as Marcus Crassus in *The Examiner,* no. 28, 8 Feb. 1711. The Elegy was first printed in the *Gentleman's Magazine,* 1764, and included in Swift's *Works,* 1765, edited by Deane Swift.

p. 98. HORACE, *Lib.* 2. *Sat.* 6 imitated. Written in the summer of 1714 just before the death of Queen Anne, when Swift had retired into the country, 'by faction tired' and despairing of any reconciliation between his 'great contending friends'.

p. 99, *l.* 35. *Lewis.* Erasmus Lewis, secretary to Harley.

p. 100, *l.* 83. *three Years and more,* a date Swift did not forget, when he was first introduced to Harley, 4 Oct. 1710.

p. 100, *l.* 94. *From Pope, from Parnel, or from Gay,* members of the Scriblerus Club, formed the previous winter in London by Dr. Arbuthnot.

p. 102. ON STELLA'S BIRTHDAY, 1718–19. The first of the series of verses addressed to Stella for her birthday on 13 Mar.; in 1719 she was in fact thirty-eight. They had first met when

Swift went to Sir William Temple in 1689, thirty years before. The verses were first printed in *Miscellanies. The Last Volume*, 1727, just after her death. Stella herself had copied them into a volume, containing a number of Swift's poems, which may be dated 1720, when he wrote to her about her collecting and transcribing his poems.

p. 102, *l.* 5. *at Sixteen,* Swift would have remembered her particularly from this time when he returned to Moor Park for his last visit to Sir William Temple from 1696 to 1699, when he 'had some share in her education, by directing what books she should read, and perpetually instructing her in the principles of honor and virtue'.

p. 102. ON STELLA'S BIRTHDAY, 1726–7. The last of the birthday verses when she was already ill, and 'for once' he offers her 'some serious Lines'. Written before his last visit to England, shortened by the news of her serious condition, which brought him back to Dublin in Sept., four months before her death.

p. 105. THE JOURNAL OF A MODERN LADY, 1729. First printed in Dublin, as *The Journal of a Dublin Lady,* it had been written at Market Hill, where it had been suggested by his hostess, Lady Acheson. The Dublin version was badly printed and this is printed from the text as corrected by Swift for *Miscellanies. The Third Volume,* 1732. A short sample only is given here, describing a ladies' evening tea-party.

p. 106. VERSES ON THE DEATH OF DR. SWIFT, 1731. Swift refers to this poem in a letter to Gay, 1 Dec. 1731: I have been several months writing near five hundred lines on a pleasant subject, only to tell what my friends and enemies will say on me after I am dead. I shall finish it soon, for I add two lines every week, and blot out four and alter eight.' It is in fact divided into paragraphs, containing one couplet, or two, or three—but chiefly four and more.

p. 106, *l.* 1. *Rochefoucault's Maxim,* no. xcix in *Reflexions ou sentences et maximes morales,* 1665, but suppressed in later editions.

p. 106, *ll.* 47 f. *Pope, Gay and Arbuthnot,* members of the Scriblerus Club, and Swift's closest friends and fellow satirists—his rivals in verse.

p. 106, *l.* 59. *St. John and Pulteney,* his closest associates in political writing—his rivals in prose.

p. 109, *l.* 305. *One quite indiff'rent in the Cause,* after describing what his friends and enemies would have to say when they heard of his death, Swift seems to have been tempted to end with a sort of Apologia—but as always uses a mask which in fact makes it possible for him to be more outspoken, and perhaps ironical at his own expense.

p. 116. THE DAY OF JUDGEMENT. This poem was first included in Swift's *Works,* and printed in the *Gentleman's Magazine,* 1775, thirty years after his death. There can be little doubt that this is the manuscript poem on the Day of Judgement which Chesterfield told Voltaire he possessed. It was first printed in *The St. James Chronicle* in 1774, when Chesterfield's *Letters* first appeared.

JOURNAL TO STELLA

p. 118. LETTER V, 30 Sept. 1710. The letters which Swift sent to Ireland during his years of political activity in London were all addressed to Mrs. Dingley, who is also included sometimes in his greetings and messages to Stella, whose regular letters to Swift were probably all destroyed. The details of his activities which fill the Journal were not only intended for the amusement of the ladies but to provide a record for future use.

p. 118, *l.* 1. *premunire,* penalty or liability, from the opening word of a writ.

p. 118, *l.* 8. *Lewis,* Erasmus Lewis, Secretary to Harley—

'a cunning Shaver
And very much in Harley's Favour.'

p. 118, *ll.* 20, 25. *Darteneuf, Lord Halifax.* Swift was still on good terms with his Whig friends.

p. 118, *l.* 22. *Tatler,* no. 230, which was concerned with 'the corruption of our English Tongue'.

p. 119, *l.* 1. *my lampoon,* on Godolphin, who had just been dismissed from the office of Treasurer.

p. 119, *l.* 13. *the cartons of Raphael,* the famous cartoons which had been bought by Charles I, and were then in the King's Gallery at Hampton Court, which had been specially designed for them by Wren.

p. 119, *l.* 33. *Presto,* pseudonym for Swift. MD seems to be used either for Stella or for the two ladies together.

p. 120, *l.* 14. *Will Penn,* the founder of Pennsylvania, then in great favour at the court of Queen Anne.

p. 120, *l.* 18. *a memorial,* in which Swift presents his case for the remission of the First Fruits for the Church of Ireland, which had been already granted by the Queen to the Church of England.

p. 120, *l.* 21. *Mr. St. John,* afterwards Viscount Bolingbroke, who had been Secretary at War in Godolphin's ministry till 1708, when he resigned with Harley, becoming Secretary of State under his ministry in 1710.

p. 121, *l.* 5. *a Tatler,* probably no. 238: *A Description of a City Shower,* see p. 95.

p. 121, *l.* 9. *you know what,* probably *A Tale of a Tub,* which had brought Swift his reputation as a powerful writer, though it had been severely censured as a dangerous work.

p. 122, *l.* 1. *Sir Andrew Fountaine,* another Whig friend of Swift's, who had been brought to Dublin by the Earl of Pembroke, when he was Lord Lieutenant of Ireland. Swift stayed at his house in Leicester Fields in 1707 and again in 1709.

p. 122, *l.* 15. *Dr. Garth,* who had written *The Dispensary* (1699), later appointed physician to George I.

p. 122, *l.* 21. *Sir John Stanley,* of county Dublin, a Commissioner of Customs, who had married Anne Granville, sister of Lord Lansdown.

p. 123. LETTER XXV. 30 June 1711. This section is a reply to Stella's letter no. 16, in which Swift allows them, and us, a glimpse of his longing to be with Stella again in the country; and a sense of his caution in building hopes of preferment in spite of his high favour with the ministry.

p. 125, *l.* 22. *Laracor,* Swift's country living, where he had a house and garden, occupied by the ladies in his absence.

p. 125, *l.* 32. *Patrick,* his servant. Footmen were allowed places in the gallery at the London theatres.

p. 127. LETTER LXIII. 12 Apr.–27 Apr. 1713. The short daily entries over this fortnight give a vivid account of the delays and difficulties in the final arrangements by which Swift received his reward and got his preferment as Dean of St. Patrick's, Dublin.

p. 129, *l.* 21. *George Berkeley,* then a Fellow of Trinity College, Dublin, had already published his *New Theory of Vision,* 1709 and *Treatise concerning the Principles of Human Knowledge*, 1710. A few months later Swift got him the appointment as Chaplain and Secretary to the Earl of Peterborough, envoy to Sicily.

p. 129, *l.* 30. *Addison's Play called Cato.* Swift had attended the rehearsal, but his account gives no indication that he had any idea how successful it would be.

p. 129, *l.* 33. *vacant Deanryes,* in England. The vacancy at St. Patrick's was due to Stearn being made a bishop. It is clear that neither the Queen nor the archbishops wanted Swift to be a bishop—or even a dean in England.

p. 130, *l.* 4. *Duke of Ormond,* then Lord Lieutenant of Ireland.

p. 131, *l.* 3. *Lady Masham,* a cousin of Harley's, much in the confidence of Queen Anne.

p. 132, *l.* 35. *Parnel & Berkeley.* Dinner with the poet and the philosopher at an alehouse was just then more to his taste than dining with ministers at Lord Dartmouth's.

p. 133, *l.* 22. *the Book I am writing,* his Memoirs of the events leading to the Treaty of Utrecht, which was only published in 1758, with the title *History of the Four Last Years of the Queen.*

p. 133, *l.* 32. *A. Bp. York.* Swift suspected that it was the Archbishop of York who was mainly responsible for his not getting a preferment in England.

p. 136. LETTER TO POPE, 29 Sept. 1725 in which Swift states his intentions in writing *Gulliver's Travels.* For a most valuable comment on this, see R. S. Crane, *The Houyhnhnms, the Yahoos, and the History of Ideas,* in *Reason and the Imagination,* Columbia University Press, 1962, pp. 231–53.

p. 136, *l.* 1. *Mr. Stopford's management,* a young Fellow of Trinity College, Dublin, who had been recommended to Pope, but had left London without seeing him.

p. 136, *l.* 16. *my Travels,* finally prepared for the printer during that summer, though Swift seems to have added some details and probably further corrections during his stay in London the next summer, 1726.

p. 136, *l.* 26. *done with translations,* Pope had just completed his work on the *Odyssey,* the last books of which were published in 1726; he had had two assistants.

p. 137, *l.* 25. *subterranean passage,* Pope's famous grotto at Twickenham.

p. 138, *l.* 10. *Dr. Arbuthnot* seems to have inspired in Swift as others a feeling of deep admiration and affection; see Letter to him, below.

p. 138, *ll.* 20–23. *Gay, Tickell, Philips,* Thomas Tickell had been secretary to Addison when he was Secretary of State, and later came over to Ireland as Secretary to Lord Carteret, the Lord Lieutenant in 1724. Ambrose Philips, the pastoral poet, had come over with Archbishop Boulter, and was writing his little flams to the daughter of the Lord Lieutenant. Swift had suggested that there would be similar opportunities for Gay.

p. 139, *l.* 5. *Bolingbroke,* at this time forty-seven, nevertheless unharmed by his fall.

p. 139. LETTER TO BENJAMIN MOTTE, the publisher of *Gulliver's Travels.*

p. 139, *l.* 9. *Mr. Hyde,* Dublin printer, who published the Dublin editions of *Gulliver's Travels.*

p. 140, *l.* 12. *Mr. Wootton,* the painter who had designed many of the plates for Gay's *Fables,* 1727.

p. 140, *l.* 35. *the poetical volume of Miscellany,* this was the 'Last' volume of the *Miscellanies* of Pope and Swift, published by Motte in 1727, and consisted wholly of verse with the exception of Pope's treatise *Of the Art of Sinking in Poetry,* which serves as a sort of preface to the volume.

p. 141. LETTER TO DR. JOHN ARBUTHNOT, NOV. 1734. Written in reply to a farewell letter dated Oct. 4, from Arbuthnot, who had been suffering from asthma and dropsy.

p. 142, *l.* 8. *the Bishop of Marseilles,* Belsunce, who in 1720 had remained in the city ministering to the victims of the plague, and had survived. Cf. Pope's *Essay on Man,* iv. 107, 8:

> Why drew Marseille's good bishop purer breath,
> When Nature sicken'd, and each gale was death?